D eciding to write this I had to take a look back at the way I viewed death then vs the way I view death as a medium.

Death is one of the hardest emotions we, as humans have to address as part of life. Let's face it we aren't getting out of here alive. No one grieves the same way. Grief come is so many forms that it can be hard to wrap your head around. How you will ever completely walk through it? Everyone confronts death at some time or another. Mourning is different every time we lose someone. The only thing that is consistent in death is that this person will no longer be able to speak to their human earthly body. Before losing my mother I viewed death in a totally different way.

Let's go back to where it started:

I'd been struggling several years with panic and anxiety attacks. Out of nowhere, they would hit. Dry heaves, cold sweats, feeling like my throat was closing up because I felt as if my tongue was swelling. Sometimes I would have tightness around my neck giving me breathing issues. We had to get rid of any clock that ticked. It made me feel like the world was closing in on me just like the end of the looney tune cartoon when the circle closes in on Porky Pig. I literally would sit on the floor between my husband's legs and have him place his hands on my shoulders because I felt as if I was leaving my body. I thought I was going crazy. Something was wrong. I am not a "go to the Doctor kinda girl" unless I have no other choice. So I went. I thought the onset of dementia, Alzheimer's, or schizophrenia. My doctor assured me that at my age it was not dementia or Alzheimer's, so off to a counselor. Diagnoses: Depression, Anxiety and PTSD. This was not a good feeling and lots of hard things that I needed to confront that I thought I already had years ago. I don't think I was suicidal but I understood why some would choose suicide to get out of this dark place. This scared the shit out of me. While going through this my Mother became sick. First the diagnosis was pneumonia then the test came back a few days later Stage IV Lung Cancer. I remember where I was when I got the call in April. I remember going into defense mode.

I needed to protect my mother and make sure she got the care she needed. Listening closely to every word the doctors said about what was going on and then saying back to the doctor what they just said to make sure I was hearing them correctly. Mom had a very short fight as she left this world June 29th at 2:11 am, 2014. Her cancer was very aggressive but I have to tell you she was so strong and I feel very lucky to have been able to be with her the night and day before she passed. We didn't say much but I felt it necessary to let her know she would be ok and that the people who came to see her got to say their last good byes. If she was asleep I'd wake her up. I didn't want her to miss an opportunity to see how deeply she was loved. We did have a conversation that when she left this earth she would have to give me signs that she was around. She smiled and said "jokes...." I love good practical jokes but from the other side? This made me pause but smile knowing she knew I needed to laugh.

We were able to bring her home where she could continue her final journey. I wasn't with my mother when she passed. I was home watching my grandson. I got the call early in the morning from my sister saying she had passed at 2:11 am. As I drove up to my mother's home probably around 2:30 in the morning a strong scent of flowers came through the open windows of my jeep. Knowing this was a sign from her, I smiled and said "I love you, mom." Not ten seconds later a wafting stench of pasture came and then quickly left and the scent of flowers surrounded me once again. I thought...you got me, you little shit. That was one of my mom's sayings.

When I arrived my mom was still in her bed with some flowers in her hands. I dropped my purse and glasses and went to her side. I leaned in and whispered things to her. As I spoke to her I felt it was important to give her a message to tell my daughter's boyfriend who had chosen to leave this world a few years before. Tell him I'm not mad at him anymore and I forgive him. It just felt important to have her relay this message.

I kissed her cheek and rubbed her hands and sang in a whisper You Are My Sunshine. This was always a song my grandmother sang to me, I sang to my kids and grandkids and my children sing it to their children. The song always made me feel loved and at home so what better thing to sing or say to my mother as we waited for the funeral home to come and take her once full of life body away.

I told you all of that for a few reasons. Soon after she passed I started seeing pillows, wall hangings, jewelry, coffee cups, and more with "You Are My Sunshine" on it. The saying was making a comeback in the market. I credit that to my mom; one of the best advertising reps in our area. While deciding to contact her estranged sister I was googling her name to find her number and I came across a post on Facebook of an older woman with dementia laying in the hospital - her loving frail husband takes her and sings, you got it, "You are my sunshine" More signs from mom. I'd wake up at 2:11 am and wonder, why would she wake me up at the time of her death? I realized later this was her new time of birth into her new chapter. I didn't realize this till a few months later.

Grieving and missing my mom was such a roller coaster of emotions but I have to tell you a pivotal event that changed my thoughts on death forever was a group reading I went to that my friend Denise was hosting in her home. I took one of my daughters with me; the daughter who had lost her boyfriend to suicide. My hope was that she'd find some closure and peace. The very first thing this medium said was You Are My Sunshine. "Are you freaking kidding me I thought?" Mom came through so strongly and gave both my daughter and myself peace.

After she was finished the reading she came to me and said, you know spirit has plans for you. This woman whom I'd never met before described my anxiety attacks, the feeling of my throat closing - everything. She advised me to either open up to spirit or close it down. Honestly, where I was emotionally, if I didn't open or close it the anxiety attacks would worsen. I almost peed myself. After coming home, talking to my husband about my experience I decided to have several conversations with God. This was so foreign to me, God chose me to do this, but He kept lining people up in my path leading me where I needed to go. Signs popped up everywhere and you know once I realized my doubt and placed it in His hands; Depression - Gone; Anxiety - Gone; ticking clocks no longer bothered me. For the first time in my life, I understood my purpose. It was not for me to question when I was being led. It was for me to follow the path. More than 5 years later, having done readings for thousands of people, Connecting to Spirit, listening to the guides I have been pushed to mentor people to open up to their God-given gifts, help others release negative thoughts around them freeing themselves from anxiety and depression. Me? A Medium? Who would have thought? Even bigger question mark; Me? A Teacher? Now, to me is scary but my guides would not let me sleep one night till I wrote down a plan to mentor and the students came. Crazy right?

One of my first mentors I was led to mentioned writing a book. Several times she would bring this up. I assumed because she was an author working on a book it was top of mind to her, so I kind of shrugged it off. To let you in on a secret, ever since I was young I said I was going to write a book. I even had a pen name because in the 70's and 80's I thought that was cool. Ready? Diane Castle. Diane is my middle name and I grew up in Greencastle, Pa. I've started several books over the years but none really came together. All of a sudden this idea came to me and here you are reading my book.

Now that death is a totally different understanding process to me why not take the things that I have consistently come up in readings from spirit, God, and my clients and put together a 30 day remembrance book.

How to walk yourself through from memories to grief back to memories. So many people tell me they are afraid they will forget. My answer is always journal it. All of my students will tell you I push journaling and setting intentions. So the intention of this book is to help you release the grief memories while journaling your memories. This will be a letter to your loved one.

My prayer is that this will help you find your new normal. It doesn't get easier; you are without someone you cared about. You find your new way to live with their memory surrounding you, a way to speak to them every day. Journal signs, dreams, songs, whatever moves you through the pain of loss to remember their legacy they left instilled in you.

I'll share a "God Wink" as I call it. While at the hospital I left the room to allow my father alone time with her. I was sitting in the waiting room looking out the window crying and praying, waiting on my sister to arrive. A man walked over to me and asked if I was ok and if there was anything he could do. I looked up and replied, "can you heal my mother?" He smiled so angelically placing his hand on my shoulder and said, "I can pray for her." With that my sister came down the hallway. We hugged, cried, and walked to her room. The stranger was no longer top of mind with me. We walked to room 3225 went and went in. A little later Dad and I walked out to give Lori time with her. When I opened the door this man was outside the door with his hands up in the air in prayer. We walked down the hallway and I looked back and he was still standing there. Now, he may have followed Lori and I to room 3225; I do not know all I know is that he was standing in prayer for someone he did not know. God was so present and He was letting me know He was there with us. As we walked to the elevator one of my dearest friends (who is no longer with us now) who works at the hospital stepped out of the elevator and looked around as if she was lost. I called her name and ran to her. She smiled and said, "I took the wrong elevator. I didn't know why but God placed me here to be with you." God winks and you just have to recognize it.

PRAISE

"Stacey is always positive...always. We met about 29 years ago. We have had our tough times just like everyone. She never gives up. We have 3 beautiful children, all grown, and they have blessed us with five grandchildren. I look at her and thank God every day that she picked me. Congratulations on your first of many books. I love you so much." - **Your husband, Jeff**

"I would like to give Special Thanks to Stacey for sharing her Spiritual gifts through Mentorship. I consider myself very lucky and honored to have met Stacey who I also call Soul Sister and friend. Divine timing put me in the right place at the right time for our meeting.

My sincere thanks to her as she took time out to help me learn to trust and believe in my own spiritual gifts/path, helping to make it easier for me to believe in myself and trust on what I am being guided. I am sure whose patience I have probably tested, but she always encouraged me to seek the inner voice.

Your famous quote: 'YOU KNOW THAT YOU KNOW, YOU KNOW?' Thank you, Stacey, for helping me release the baggage I carried around from past traumas and lives so I can move forward in love for myself and others. THANK YOU!" - *Tammy F.*

"From my experience, here is what I can say about Stacey - she is absolutely amazing and extraordinary!! I had such an incredible reading with her that I went on to join her mentoring program to help me explore my own possible talents and gifts. To my surprise, she started me with the 'grass roots' of knowing thyself and connecting, and did I struggle with the many exercises given. Stacey was so patient, kind and thorough in her teachings and allowed me to go at my own pace. Her mentoring had stirred up

pretty much ALL my insecurities big time, and I realized that I had much inner work to do yet before expressing my abilities out there. Stacey gave me a foundation to work with and thus activated my now known abilities, as I continue to do the inner work and expand my level of consciousness.

What stands out the most to me about Stacey, is truly her Spirit and Heart. For when it comes to real-life situations, like when I reached out to her later, Stacey not only rose to the occasion of my call for help, but she also went 'above and beyond the call of duty'. I had a dreaded decision to make with my beloved boy cat, Max, who had cancer and appeared ready to move on. Stacey not only communicated effectively with Max while on a road trip far away, but she also helped prepare me for what would be next in his transition - peace for both of us - absolutely phenomenal! I am so humbled and grateful to Stacey for her Divineness."
- *Gudrun S.*

"I am so grateful I participated in Stacey's mentoring program. She shared with me tools and knowledge that allowed me to tap into my higher knowing. I also gained a camaraderie with like-minded individuals who were on a similar spiritual path. Her mentorship opened my mind to the possibility that I could access parts of my being I didn't know were hidden. I have since been traveling a path of growth and harmony." - *Clara H.*

"I met Stacey when I scheduled a private reading. I had lost my mother and was devastated. I was praying she would be able to communicate with my mom and was so thrilled when she did. The things she was able to tell me were amazing. Then she said, "You know you can do this." I told her I had always wanted to. She told me about her mentor and how much they helped her. A few weeks

later, I thought about what she said and started to look for classes and people I could learn from. Then I called Stacey and made another appointment for a private reading. After our second reading, I asked her if she would mentor me, and she said YES! I was so happy and excited because I had finally found someone I could learn from. I really wanted to communicate with spirit and help others like Stacey helped me. We have worked together closely together for about two years and she has helped me open my mind and shown me how to read signs. Stacey's knowledge and abilities are amazing, and I could not have found a better mentor. I now can understand when spirit comes through and gives me messages. It is such an amazing feeling to be able to give someone messages from spirit and help them heal. I am grateful for Stacey taking my spiritual journey with me." - *Tina A.*

"I was very hesitant about going with my daughter because I did not think that someone could really connect with a spirit. From the moment I stepped into the room, I felt very welcomed and comfortable. This woman knew NOTHING about me, she had written down that I was joining my daughter. I was instantly in tears when my father came out and the things that were said. He was actually there, and I still am shaken, not only because he came to talk, but this was so WOW. I definitely recommend this woman...you won't regret it!!!" - *Audra A.*

"I went to a group reading with Stacey. There were smiles, laughter and tears in the room, not tears of sadness so much but of understanding and gratefulness in knowing our loved ones are still with us and they know what is on our heart. The messages I received pertained to me perfectly.

PRAISE

Stacey's God-given gift is amazing. My son, Harry, said it was life-changing for him as he learned so many of the details previously unknown to him. She even had a message for his sister who did not join us, and it was spot on. Our angel cards were spot on as well and rang true. We both look forward to having a one-on-one with Stacey and attending more group readings. She is a true spiritual healer with a gift." - *Tracey S.*

"Stacey is the most down to earth kindhearted woman I've ever met! I wasn't 100% sure what to expect going into my first reading to connect to the spirits, but overall, this was the best experience. We connected with my grandpa & my brother and then my cards were a huge eye-opener. I highly recommend her for your spiritual needs! 10/10 stars will be coming again in the future. She literally is a gift from God." ♥♥♥*Sierra A.*

"I just listened to one of your Tuesday Talks at 10:30 am and was touched by your personal connection and your own journey that brought you to be the compassionate healer and bright soul that you are today. I listened to it this morning when praying, and I felt inner peace, love, and gratitude. Thank you, Stacey, for opening up your life to others, for your deep connections, and for connecting me to spirit." - *Theresa B.*

"I was amazed at Stacey's skills as a medium. Just being in the room with her lifted my spirits and released the heaviness inside me. She truly does talk to our loved ones who have passed, with no prompting or gimmicks. She is truly a soulful being and talks to all spirits that are reaching out. So very worth the money for a 60 - minute reading. She has changed my life for the better." ♥
- *Vanessa B.*

PRAISE

"I had a live reading with Stacey, and it was enlightening and wonderful. We laughed, cried and connected. I felt so cleansed and invigorated afterward. My fears were put into perspective, and she gave me hope. Can you think of a better way to come away from this? If you are on the fence, consider Stacey, she is very open, welcoming and kind." - *Kris E.*

"I have had several readings done by different mediums, but Stacey is the only one I've ever returned to for multiple sessions. She has a true gift and is able to effectively communicate my spirit guides messages in a way that resonates with me deeply. She's also presented messages from my passed loved ones in such a loving and reassuring way, which I appreciate fully. The atmosphere she creates feels safe, relaxing and calming. She is down to earth and overall a great person to converse with in general. I will always recommend Stacey." - *Anna B.*

"Speaking with Stacey felt so incredibly comfortable. I felt right at home and welcome by her the second we first spoke. Our session was filled with revelations I feel like I've known but couldn't face for whatever reason. I'm grateful for finally taking the time to reach out and schedule a session with her. Her gift is a true blessing!" - *Samantha R.*

"Stacey is always spot on. She literally changed my life! I recommend a reading or two or three... I also recommend booking an Energy Healing appointment." - *Nicole Z.*

"I went to one of the butterfly release group readings with my husband. I wasn't sure what to expect but must say that Stacey is the most genuine person with a beautiful gift. My mother-in-law came through in our reading and provided us with reassurance and closure.

It was such a special experience, and I highly recommend her to anyone looking to connect with spirits. I look forward to seeing her again sometime in the future." - *Rita B.*

"I had an amazing reading with Stacey. She is so kind and inviting. She made me feel right at home. She started by explaining her intentions and what spirit and angels do. She encouraged any questions I had during the reading. My mother, grandmother, and a very close friend came through. She said things that no one should have known about. I got so much helpful and insightful information from her that has really answered a lot of questions for me and is helping me to heal. Finally, I had the closure that I longed for. I would have a reading with Stacey a thousand times over. Thank you, Stacey, for the answers and healing that I was seeking." - *Courtney S.*

"Ten Blazing Stars... Stacey is a true Rebel Earth Angel with a God-given gift that connects us to communicate far beyond our reach. The curious were astounded and the skeptics made believers. Those ready to receive got what they wanted and more. We cried, we laughed, we grew together, all of us. Thank you, Sister!" ♥ - *Kelly H.*

"Stacey changed my life. Her mentorship opened the path for me to find my purpose and awakened my soul. I have accomplished things I would never have dreamed of opening my heart and mind to visualize. There is nothing I cannot overcome. I will always be grateful to her for sharing her knowledge and spirit with me."
- *Heidi D.*

For information about permission to reproduce selections from this book, write to:
Stacey Niedentohl
2168 Mont Alto Rd.
Chambersburg, PA 17202
717 552 1840
ConnectingToSpiritwithStacey@gmail.com
ConnectingtoSpiritwithStacey.com

Published by Connecting to Spirit Publishing
Library of Congress Control Number: 2021914587

Paperback ISBN 978-1-0879-0841-0
eBook ISBN: 978-1-0879-7679-2

Printed in the United States of America.

This book, although therapeutic in nature, does not replace therapy or any form of treatment in which you are engaged. Individuals with medical or psychological problems should consult their physician or therapist before engaging in the exercises of this book to discuss modifications relevant to their unique circumstances and conditions. The author of this book does not dispense medical advice nor prescribe the use of any technique as a form of treatment for physical, emotional or medical problems without the advice of a physician or primary therapist. The intent of the author is only to offer information of a general nature in your quest for emotional and spiritual well-being. In the event you use any of the information in this book for yourself, the author and the publisher assume no responsibility for your actions.

DEDICATION & ACKNOWLEDGMENTS

This book is dedicated to the many people who have touched and influenced my life.

First and foremost, our Lord and Savior who with Him all things are possible. I have full faith that He is guiding me through every step of my journey.

The loved ones who have gone before me and continue to show me their insight from the other side.

My mom "Darlene Haugh" who taught me strength comes in all forms. I didn't realize how strong she was until she was no longer by my side.

My father-in-law "Jerry Niedentohl" who taught me never to waste a good story. The man was a great storyteller.

My Uncle Glenn, who walked this earth for 99 years, 2 months and 28 days, who taught me age is just a number. Never get old. And to always say I love you. He would always tell me, "I love you. You are my very best friend."

My forever friends:

Deb Mumma who taught me what a badass really is; never allowing the "c" word (cancer) to control her thoughts.

Rick Debo who taught me always to smile. His last message to me was, "I promised the good Lord to make people smile and laugh as long as He keeps me here and I'm having fun doing it."

Ty Long who taught me about interactive cowboy cooking. There is nothing like a chocolate cake made over an open fire shared with good friends.

DEDICATION & ACKNOWLEDGMENTS

My earthly support team:

Denise Aulton who acts as my friend/counselor, booking agent/manager, cheerleader/promoter and soul sister. Without her guidance and support, I would not be where I am today.

All my clients who trust me to humbly deliver messages from their loved ones. Each reading touches my heart and soul differently. I feel more blessed with each reading.

My kids Dustyn, Megan and Randi. Grand kids: Kailey, Eli, Dillinger, Tiernan and Marley who have been on this journey with me. Imagine living as children and grandchildren of a Medium. They are my world.

And last but not least, my loving and supportive husband of 26 years, Jeff. Without his love and moral support, this book and what I do would not be possible. I can honestly say I am married to the best husband in the world! "Yer Dynamite, Babe!"

All these people and so many others too numerous to mention have helped me to stay true to my intention. "To inspire and help as many people as possible walk through that part of their life that needs help in healing. To have them say and feel - because of something you said, I did not give up."

I pray you all "Love the life you live and live the life you love...."
- Bob Marley

Blessings

Stacey

MY HEAD KNOWS

*BUT MY HEART STILL HURTS

A 30 - DAY GRIEF RECOVERY JOURNAL

STACEY NIEDENTOHL

DAY ONE
THE LINK THAT FORMED THE CHAIN

What makes a chain strong? We all know from learning in school, each link is attached to the next and then to the next. Sometimes, a link gets old, and a crack forms. This represents disease of the human body. Sometimes the chain breaks. This represents the death of the missing link in the once strong chain. The chain will never be the same. This once strong chain is now missing an important link. Now, the chain can come together and mend with the links that are left. These links are the family and friends that were all connected by this one person who is no longer on this earth. This link cannot be replaced by another link, but the other links can form a strong bond that can hold the rest of the chain together (family and friends). Alone these links are just a circle but can create strength when entwined with the others. What can you add to the chain to make it strong again?

- Memories
- Pictures
- Stories
- Sayings they said
- Continuing traditions
- Starting a new tradition in their honor

Place one of your favorite pictures here that would represent a link in the chain.

Place a Photo Here

- 16 -

PAUSE...BREATHE...WRITE

Write what you remember about the day the picture was taken.

PAUSE...BREATHE...WRITE

Mantra: *Today I am reconnected.*

WHO AM I?

Once you lose someone that was a permanent fixture of your life for a long time, you may look in the mirror and think,
Who am I without them? It can be a very confusing time. You've lost someone who made you who you are. Your identity has been changed drastically. If you are like me, you always knew someday they would not be around, but for it to now be the reality of life a lot of deep breaths are needed.

Here is what I want you to remember. They are still part of you. The memories you have, the things you've learned from them, are still with you. If they were a parent or grandparent, they are still bone of your bone and flesh of your flesh. Their genes are coursing through your body. They are still part of you. Just as fabric has separate threads, the threads are still part of the piece of material. The same goes for you.

It feels and looks different, but your loved one would want you to continue in their memory. When Mom passed, I still have the urge to call her from time to time. She was my mom for 49 years. How does a daughter go on without her mother? How do I as a mother console my children and grandchildren? These are questions that run through my mind like a mouse on a wheel. I started to compare us. Remembering things she said and did. Who would she want me to be or do? She would not want me to feel motherless, because she would want her life to impact my life until my last breath.

God Wink:

As a reminder that I am bone of her bone, I had an "aha" moment slap me in the face. I have her wedding rings that I wear. I have a love of jewelry. One day, I only had my engagement ring on with her wedding set. I put my hand up to push open a door, and I saw my mom's hand. I have her hands. I know it may sound odd, but my hands look exactly like her hands and I never really noticed till that moment. Bone of my bone and flesh of my flesh. Mom's hands are my hands, her hands are mine. That is who I am right now. When days are tough, I see her hands in mine. She is helping me by holding my hand. That's all I need for now. That is who I am. She is giving me a hand, holding my hand every day, every minute, every second.

Start to think, who am I? What part of them is with me, helping me?

PAUSE...BREATHE...WRITE

 Mantra: *I am in them, and they are in me*

Who am I without you?

Who am I without you?
I'm just not sure, what I'm to do.
In the blink of the eye, my life has changed
what once was normal is now rearranged.

The air and sun just are not the same.
How do I respond to life's brand-new game?
My heartbeat is different my head is a mess.
I can barely get up to get showered or dressed.

My questions are many,
the answers are few
confusion and whirlwinds
of just what to do.

But I hear your voice saying
in my head it's replaying.
Your whisper in my ear,
I'm within you, my dear.

MISSING VS. REMEMBERING

In speaking with clients, they always mention things they miss. I asked my clients to give me a list of things they miss. I recommend changing the way you look at it. Say, "I remember." See how it changes.

- I miss your guidance and laughter
- I remember you always gave me the best advice, and you had the best laugh
- I miss just knowing you are here
- I remember you were always there for me
- I miss the comfort you gave me
- I remember you always knew what to say to give me comfort
- I miss everything about you
- I remember everything about you
- I miss how loved you made me feel
- I remember no matter what, you made me feel loved
- I miss you telling me you were proud of me
- I remember you were always proud of me
- I miss the smell of your skin
- I remember the smell of your skin
- I miss our phone calls
- I remember all the times we spoke on the phone
- I miss you calling me by my nickname
- I remember the nickname you gave me
- I miss being in the same room as you
- I remember you sitting on the couch beside me
- I miss your morning kiss and you texting me
- I remember you always kissed me in the morning, and you would text me just because
- I miss your sense of humor
- I remember your sense of humor
- I miss your voice

MISSING VS. REMEMBERING

- I remember how I just needed to hear your voice to know everything would be ok
- I miss your hugs
- I remember you gave me the best hugs
- I miss your friendship
- I remember our friendship. You are my forever friend.
- I miss going out to dinner
- I remember all the times we went out to dinner
- I miss hearing I love you
- I remember how you always told me you loved me
- I miss your silly stories
- I remember you told the silliest stories
- I miss your smile and the way you looked at me
- I remember how you smiled when you looked at me

It is normal to miss them. But missing something makes it seem like it was taken away, never to be had again. Remember, it is a gift they gave you, memories that will be with you forever. Now, you try it. What do you miss?

PAUSE...BREATHE...WRITE

PAUSE...BREATHE...WRITE

PAUSE...BREATHE...WRITE

PAUSE...BREATHE...WRITE

Now take those same things and start with "I remember." Be specific, go into detail. Show your gratitude for the memories they gave to you. I remember...

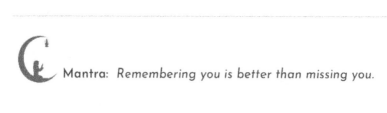

Mantra: *Remembering you is better than missing you.*

FEELINGS OF LOSS - THE BIG SEVEN

They say there are seven stages of grief. Below are some feelings we all share. I think we can all agree that there are many emotions we go through from when you first heard they passed to a month after, one year, five years and later, birthdays, anniversaries, etc. We all have triggers that bring waves of emotions that sometimes feel as though we are drowning. I've added a few more that I, myself, have gone through. There is no time limit for grief. There is no appointment with grief. It shows up when we least expect it. Be gentle with yourself and allow yourself to walk through what you need to heal your heart.

I hope this list helps you identify you are not alone in grief.

- Devastation
- Overwhelmed
- Feeling unable to stand on your own two feet
- Fear of letting yourself go
- Shock
- Reality is different
- Anxiety
- Worrying about your own mortality
- Anger and Irritation
- Hopelessness
- Fear of going to bed, fear of getting out of bed
- Stress
- Exhaustion
- Loss of appetite/overeating for comfort
- Panic Attacks
- Nightmares
- Constant thoughts of the person who passed
- Questions and confusion
- Hard to think. Hard to stop thinking.
- Asking for signs. Am I missing the signs?
- Blame

FEELINGS OF LOSS - THE BIG SEVEN

- Loneliness
- Can't make decisions or making hasty decisions
- Hard to be around people/fear of being alone
- What is my life worth living without them
- Will it ever really get better
- Numbness/feelings of emptiness
- Other memories of loss
- Forgetfulness
- Spiritual beliefs change
- Nothing seems important
- Comparing yourself with how others are getting through it
- Feelings of going crazy
- Hearing and seeing things
- Confusion and disorientation
- Low energy/super energy
- Searching for meaning
- Feeling sick
- Relief, then guilt for feeling relief
- Emptiness
- Fear
- Disconnection
- Responsibility
- Regret
- Are they okay, and where are they
- Were they afraid, alone, in pain
- Did I do everything they needed me to do

Mantra: *I allow myself to grieve in my own way.*

No worries of tomorrow

Today I will slow down
As I breathe in and as I breathe out
Today I will listen to loud music and dance all around
As I breathe in and as I breathe out
Today I will be grateful for me and all my accomplishments
As I breathe in and as I breathe out
Just for today the scent of fresh air will make me smile
As I breathe in and as I breathe out
Just for today I will not allow something to steal my joy
As I breathe in and as I breathe out
Just for today I will notice the signs you send me, look up
and smile, thanking you and ask you to send me more
As I breathe in and as I breathe out
Just for today I will remember good memories
and feel the warmth of your love surrounding me
As I breathe in and as I breathe out
Just for today I will not criticize myself or others
As I breathe in and as I breathe out
Just for today I will show myself honor and grace
As I breathe in and as I breathe out
Just for today I will not quit or give up on me or others
As I breathe in and as I breathe out
Just for today I will realize there are 24 hours in a day
...no more...no less
As I breathe in and as I breathe out
Just for today colors will be brighter
and I will notice them in love
As I breathe in and as I breathe out
Just for today when I speak to a child I will kneel down
and look in their eyes in wonderment
As I breathe in and as I breathe out
And when I lay in my bed tonight I will note
that I lived just for today
As I breathe in and as I breathe out
Knowing that tomorrow
I will live just for today
As I breathe in and as I breathe out

NOW IT'S IMPORTANT

Grief comes in waves. There will be bad days and good days. Days you won't know how to breathe. Days filled with memories some will make you laugh, while others; will bring tears.

With each day a different wave will come in and go out. When the good days come, don't feel bad that you feel good. Different things will remind you of them. Pictures, smells, phone calls, running into friends. Things that you never thought would matter to you.

God Wink:

Every year I host Thanksgiving. Every year, Mom would say she would bring the napkins. It always made me laugh...napkins, why napkins? I remember my husband saying to me that one day you're going to miss her bringing the napkins. Then, the napkins just seemed unimportant. I mean, they are napkins. But it was special to her. She would find different ones each year. Turkeys, pilgrims, pumpkins or cornucopia, oh my...After she passed, I was shopping with my sister at a local gift shop. It was June, and there in the clearance corner were napkins with turkeys on them. As I picked them up with tears in my eyes, I just had to buy them. The once unimportant napkins brought back memories of her voice on the phone. I could not leave the store without buying all they had. All 5 packs were mine.

Write about something that once seemed unimportant, but now is an homage to your loved one's legacy.

PAUSE...BREATHE...WRITE

 Mantra: *Today I will allow the waves to wash over me.*

SIGNS

"You are my Sunshine...Please don't take my sunshine away."

Signs are those Oh-My-Gosh moments. Goosebumps and tingles that you just can't explain. At the time, you are so overwhelmed, feeling that your loved one is near you. But later your brain tries to rationalize that, "Oh, I miss them so much, I'm making this up." Have you been there in your head when the human part of the brain tries to talk you out of what your intuition knows to be true? We both know you have.

Most common signs from spirit are butterflies, dragonflies, feathers, cardinals, songs, lights flickering, scents, ladybugs, flowers, numbers, rainbow, pennies, nickels, dimes, radio and television signal static, candles suddenly blown out, etc.

Different signs that spirit has mentioned are nuts & bolts, bells ringing, wind chimes moving without wind or just the sound of wind chimes, strumming from guitars, hearts in clouds, a rainbow over the house they were visiting, feeling like someone is sitting on their bed beside them.

God Wink:

My mom is awesome with sending me feathers, but this past Christmas Day blew me away. She loved Christmas. Every year she would wear these earrings that I bought for her when I was young, maybe second grade. I have a small box of her Christmas jewelry. The week of Christmas I looked in the box to put them on to wear them and they were not there. I know I looked at least ten times; I even emptied the box, and no earrings. I was heartbroken, not knowing what I had done with them. I got up Christmas morning and something told me to look one more time. It's not a big box, they probably aren't there, but I looked anyway. I opened the box, and there they were, both together on top of all the other earrings and pins. You probably wonder how I missed them. I didn't. She only wore them on Christmas day. I was looking for them too soon.

SIGNS

I know she found them and led me to look one more time. Christmas morning, I cried as I put these clip-on earrings on my ears. This was my fifth Christmas without her. But I was wearing her earrings.

PAUSE...BREATHE...WRITE

What was the sign your loved one sent you? What were you doing and where were you?

Mantra: *Today I will be a sign that you were loved.*

Signs

Your body had transitioned into spirit's rebirth,
With all the stars wrapped in the colors of earth
from the glow of the sun
to the clock showing "One: One: One"
I see you; I feel you; I know you are near.
Send me a sign so it's perfectly clear.

A message in a song
that helps me be strong
A feather in my car,
You sent me a falling star,
I ask for a sign and they appear
It makes things feel better; it releases my fear.

When the scent of your perfume seems to linger
My entire body is covered in tingles
Red birds in the trees that don't want to leave
I smile to myself, and whisper, I believe
Your essence embraces my spirit now and then
through memories within me and the signs that you send.

We are going to go deep into the heart today. Go to the warm feeling you had when you were together. There are just certain things people do and say that show how much we mean to them. My forever friend (Deb) who was like a sister to me knew just what to say and how to say it. It didn't matter if it had been a week or a year since we spoke. She was there when I needed her. She was one of the few people who could put me in my place when I needed it.

God Wink:

When Mom was close to the end, Deb came to her hospital room (she worked in the hospital). She walked into Mom's room, checked her feet, and asked the nurse to bring a warm blanket for them. Deb walked up to her side, touched her face, looked into her eyes, and told her, "You know you raised an amazing daughter." My mom smiled and said, "I did my best." Deb smiled and said, "You did a great job." My forever friend always knew what to say. Even when she had to tell me I was not being reasonable and to rethink what I was about to say to her when I was ready to respond. That statement and the look on her face would always make me laugh. I always thought that out of the two of us, I was the badass. Turns out she was the badass. She was one of the strongest women I know, and she was always there for me.

What made you feel loved?

Mantra: *Today I will pay it forward.*

When someone dies, we roll around in our head those things we should have said. Not always with regret, but we wish we would have said more. We always feel like there is plenty of time.

But we soon find out that there were missed opportunities. Always take the time to tell others you love them, compliment them, say you are proud of them, etc. Even if we take these opportunities, there is always something we feel we could have relayed to them. In this journal entry, I'm asking you to write them a letter. Tell them all the things you love and admire about them, big or small. Have the conversation with them from your heart to your pen to this journal page.

God Wink:

This one is a bit difficult for me. I'm not always great at telling friends and family I love them or I'm proud of them. It comes easily when it's my husband, kids and grandkids but for others, it is more difficult for me. I'm a work in progress. However, this is not about that. Before my mom was diagnosed with cancer, I noticed she was losing weight. A good bit of weight, but I said nothing. Mom had mentioned that she was losing weight without really trying, but she was happy that she had lost some pounds. She struggled with her weight for years, so it should have been a red flag to me. I should have questioned it, but I did not. I missed an opportunity to find out why her body was just getting rid of weight. Would it have changed things? Maybe, but probably not. I'm a firm believer that God had a plan for her. Not one that I liked, but a plan. Nothing I could have done would have made a difference. But maybe, just maybe, in her mind she thought if I hadn't questioned it, then there was nothing for her to be concerned about. My missed opportunity of saying something to my mom.

Things I didn't have a chance to say to you. Take the time now:

Mantra: *Today I will write you a letter.*

There are so many memories that we carry with us. Sometimes memories show up as tears because we are so thankful for having this person in our lives. After our loved one passes we so often think, I wish I would have said thank you.

God Wink:

When my father-in-law passed, there were so many people who showed up to honor and remember Jerry. He was one of the best storytellers ever. Oh, and the stories everyone told, there were so many. I had not been to many funerals where there was laughter. But we laughed and cried all day. I had never spoken at a funeral, but everyone was getting up to speak, so I decided to go up and say something. It had never really hit me until that very moment that his influence on my husband made him the man he was. He created the man that I have been happily married to for over twenty-five years -the way he respected his wife and women in general, the way he took care of things, his love of music, his sense of humor, his storytelling, his laugh...I see it all inside his son. When he wasn't looking...I noticed. Thank you for being the man you were and teaching my husband to respect women, and love and respect his wife and family.

PAUSE...BREATHE...WRITE

PAUSE...BREATHE...WRITE

In the space below write your loved one a thank you note.

Mantra: *I am thankful for the time I had with you.*

I Didn't Get to Tell You

I didn't get to tell you
just what you meant to me
those moments we were together
are deep inside of me

I didn't get to tell you
how much I loved your hugs
To feel your arms around me
a chance for one more hug

I didn't get to tell you
I loved to hold your hand.
To feel I was protected
I'd reach out for your hand

I didn't get to tell you
I loved to hear you laugh
I recall your stories
And tell them and others laugh

I didn't get to tell you
I saw when you weren't looking
the special things you did for me
Now you're watching when I'm not looking

I didn't get to tell you
Your life among your flowers
but now you send the scents of them
I can smell your favorite flowers

I didn't get to tell you
you were a great human being
your laugh, your touch, your smile
I admired your very being

I didn't get to tell you
I miss you saying goodbye
You'd watch me leave beside the door
I didn't want to say goodbye

T oday is about closing your eyes and envisioning them in front of you. The color of their eyes, the scent of their skin, the warmth of their hand, how they walked and talked. The things, that made them unique.

God Wink:

 On the fifth anniversary of Mom's death, my friend Denise told me to do something my mother always did in order to celebrate her. Mom's toes were always painted red. That day, I went out and bought red nail polish. A friend of mine that owns a salon just popped in. I believe Mom sent Elaine to paint my toes so they would look like hers. Every time I looked at them, I smiled and thought, Mom is walking with me today.

PAUSE...BREATHE...WRITE

Describe something about your loved one that makes you smile when you see, hear or smell it.

PAUSE...BREATHE...WRITE

Mantra: *Today I will do something that you always did and know that you are watching.*

PAUSE...BREATHE...WRITE

Mantra: *Today I will do something that you always did and know that you are watching.*

*T*he shock of hearing that someone has passed affects all of us differently. Some of us instantly break down. If you're like me, you clean and go into defense mode. I have to get things done.

However, you respond to death, permit yourself to go through the emotions. There is no correct response. Be gentle with yourself. Allow it to sink in. Give yourself time.

God Wink:

One of my high school friends that I'll speak about in this book several times passed away a few years ago. He lived in Florida, but we kept in touch with late-night messages. He didn't sleep well, and I am a night owl. I remember on the day before I had heard of his passing I was very anxious. Something wasn't right. Because I am a medium, my guides give me signs and messages. To me, it is the protective energy my guides place around me, which results in the anxiety I feel. I kept thinking something wasn't right, but I couldn't figure it out. The next evening, I received a message from a high school friend. The message simply said, "Can I call you?" It was maybe 8 p.m. She lives in the Carolinas, and I thought it was odd that she would ask. I messaged back, "Of course." The phone rang ten seconds later. She knew Debo and I had always been close. He had passed, and she didn't want me to find out through Facebook. I was sitting on our porch when she called and told me. I instantly stood up, moved things around and started to clean. I knew there were a few friends I needed to call, so they were given the same respect Sharon had given me. I remember it like yesterday. I lost a friend, a brother, someone who got me out of as much trouble as we got into during school. I miss his late-night messages and re-read them often.

In this journal entry, we are going to go back to the time you heard. Remember to be easy on yourself. If you are not ready, know that is okay if you need to come back to this day later.

If you were with them, explain their journey that you witnessed. Where you were, what you said, what did they say, did you notice anything as their spirit left? Who was there, etc.? If you were not with them, how did you hear? Where were you? Who told you?

Write about any signs or feelings you have about the day they passed.

PAUSE...BREATHE...WRITE

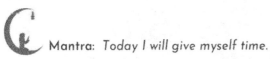

Mantra: *Today I will give myself time.*

Where the Earth meets the Sky

There wasn't much time to tell you goodbye

Because you were gone in the blink of an eye,

I know you are flying with your angels up high

Where I know that all rainbows meet the earth to the sky.

W e all have memories of the last time we saw our loved one. We replay it repeatedly in our minds. We often think I should have said this to them. I never thanked them for... But instead, let's recall the wonderful things of the last time you spoke.

God Wink:

 I write and often speak of my Uncle Glenn. A genuine hero that loved God and his country. He had a tremendous impact on my life. Before he passed, he had spent some time in the hospital for pneumonia.

At 99 years old, I thought this would perhaps be what takes him home. I spoke to him several times while he was in the hospital. He just wanted to come home. I spoke with him on a Friday and had talked him into staying in over the weekend, only to receive a phone call from the nurse saying they could release him. Once he was home, I called and asked if he'd like me to bring him dinner. He loved Italian food (he called it eye - talian). I took him some spaghetti and meatballs, and we sat and watched the football game with his son, Barry. He was so busy eating his food that he didn't realize the commentators were speaking in Spanish. They would say Ay yay yay. I laughed and said, "Did you want that in Spanish." He bellowed, "What?" So, I repeated it. He messed with the remote, then just waved his hand and turned the volume down. When I left, he grabbed my hand like always and said, "Oh honey; I love you." He was hospitalized again about two weeks later because of his heart. I wasn't able to see him before he passed, but my heart goes to the dinner we had at his home. I am so thankful for that last dinner, which I feared would not happen when he was hospitalized for pneumonia. I can picture it in my mind so clearly, and it makes me smile.

Bonus God Wink:

My poppy passed away when I was two or three. I have very few memories of him. I remember he used to climb the fruit trees and pick apples for us. My last memory was of him climbing an apple tree. I don't remember him coming down, so in my inexperienced childlike eyes, I thought he climbed up to heaven.

PAUSE...BREATHE...WRITE

Below, jot down what you remember about your last talk. Try to remember where you were, what you were wearing, things you said - every detail. Find the blessings. If the conversation did not go well, write what you wish you had said. If you need to apologize or offer forgiveness, write it down. Whatever you need to say about your last conversation, journal it and release it.

PAUSE...BREATHE...WRITE

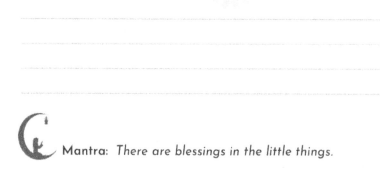

Mantra: *There are blessings in the little things.*

I Asked God

I asked God if he would allow you to stay
But He had other plans for you on that day
I thanked God for all the memories we shared
Even the moments when I was scared

I asked God why He took you away
When I felt that you wanted to stay
I thanked God for your love and your grace
and your beautiful smile that lit up your face

I asked God to take good care of you
He smiled, and He said, what else would I do
I thank God for the life you've lived
for the kindness you shared and the love that you give

I asked God to meet you at Heaven's Gate
He smiled, and He said He would not be late
I thanked God for taking away all your pain
And He promised, one day I'd see you again

ou know, now it is called a celebration of life. It is no longer referred to as a funeral. I never really got that till someone very close to me passed away. I wanted to celebrate them. I wanted to hear other people's stories and memories. It made me smile to see how many people came to talk about how they changed or touched the lives of others. I realized it wasn't just about me and my loss. It was about you and how your memory will live on.

God Wink:

On the day of Mom's celebration of life, I remember thinking people just don't know what to say as they wait to walk up to hug me. Oh my gosh! How many people do I have to hug? What's the appropriate number of hugs for this day to be over? I'm sure it was as awkward for them as it was for me. Looking at the pictures of her life through the years, one man stood out to me. He knew exactly what to say. I can still see his face as he spoke to me. My Uncle Bill, a very tall, hardworking man, looked me in the eye, tapped his heart and only said, "You know." I will always remember that. I don't remember much of that day. It is a blur, but his deep voice and icy blue eyes said more to me than anyone else. His eyes and heartfelt "you know" while tapping his heart with two of his fingers. This meant the most to me and was the best thing anyone could express to me.

PAUSE...BREATHE...WRITE

It may be a foggy memory but reflect on what you remember. Who came that I did not expect to see? What was something that was said about them I want to remember?

PAUSE...BREATHE...WRITE

Mantra: *Today is about you and the life that you shared with everyone who loved you.*

We only know one side of our loved one. The one they let us in on. We only know that person. We don't always know what they mean to others. As human beings, we have several sides to our personality. How they've touched so many lives in so many ways. I love to hear stories from others about my mom, my uncle, or others who have passed. How they impacted more people than we realized. Things they did that surprised you and touched your heart. My God Wink is one that surprised me.

God Wink:

 I always want to keep the memory of my mom's sense of humor alive. She had the biggest smile and the greatest laugh. A story that I remember was from my niece who said to me, "Grandma is the first person who swore at me." It shocked me because my mom did not have the sailor mouth like I do. So, I said, "What?" She said "Yep, she looked at me, smiled, pointed her finger at me, and said, 'You little shit.' And we were in church!!" That was always Mom's go-to line when you caught her on something.

Today, I'd like you to think about the stories that you heard. How they touched others. If you don't have a story, ask members of their family or friends what their favorite memory was of your person. I have lots I could have used as a God Wink but my mom was notorious for saying "You little shit." I believe sometimes it is healing to hear others tell about the person they knew. It helps us to understand the total person, not just the personality you knew.

Mantra: *Today I will think about the you I did not know and all the lives you touched.*

We'll Meet on the Mountain

You taught me to love
how to care and forgive
I look at your picture
to memories relived

I learned from your death
not to take life for granted
I've blossomed and grown
from the seeds that you planted

What you left in my heart
will never die
though you're no longer with me
This isn't goodbye

We'll meet on that mountain
beneath the moonlight
I know you'll be waiting
for my angel flight.

Traveling with someone whether on vacation or just to the store can create everlasting memories. At the time, they may not seem important but as time goes by they grow to be an implanted snapshot in your mind. You remember expressions your loved one always used or their body language.

God Wink:

One year, our vacation was to Busch Gardens and Mom was not someone who went on the rides. We talked her into going on the Loch Ness Monster, a roller coaster. We told her it wasn't bad. I remember getting in line and thinking she is going to be so mad. Sitting on the ride before we took off, taking one last look back at her before she found out what she was in for. Needless to say, she was not happy with us after the ride. I believe her words were, "You little shits."

Place a
Photo
Here

PAUSE...BREATHE...WRITE

Today I want you to recall somewhere you went, add a picture if you have one. Describe a memory of a place you went to together. Why was it important?

Mantra: *Today I will take you on a ride with me.*

I n life, we all have embarrassing moments. Some of us more than others, but we are all human and that is part of what makes us who we are. At that moment, you may have felt as though you wanted to climb into a hole, never to been seen again. Once time goes by, it turns into another memory to catalog as special.

God Wink:

My husband's Uncle Heinz was a tall, gruff-voiced man. We'd drive to Virginia Beach with the kids to visit. He always made room for us. One morning, while we were still in bed, there was a light tap on the bedroom door; the door opened, and this loud gruff voice said to Jeff, "You wanna go yard saling?" I was a bit surprised. Here I am lying in bed asleep figuring the soft knock was one of my kids and in walks my uncle. He was such a gem. The voice was very intimidating, but the man had a heart of gold.

PAUSE...BREATHE...WRITE

Write it down as though you are speaking to your loved one. Think of a moment that at the time may have been uncomfortable, but now it is a blessing in your memory.

PAUSE...BREATHE...WRITE

Mantra: *Today I will Laugh with Joy.*

Make No Mistake
Today.... So Far Away

I went to call you today
But you can't answer, you are too far away
Today, I felt your kiss on my face
It was the sun & God's loving grace
Today, I held a photo of you in your Easter Dress
Having had you in my life, I feel so blessed
Today, I smelled your perfume in the air
Me without you seems so unfair
Today, I laid your blanket across my legs
To hear your laugh again, oh how I beg
Today, I thought I saw your face
Looking again, it wasn't the case
Today, I listened to an old voicemail
I heard every word, every breath, and every detail
And in the morning when I wake
Make no mistake
I'll go to call you today
But you're in heaven, so far away

*l*aughter is the best cure for anything and everything. When in doubt...laugh. It not only releases tension, but it also raises your vibration and makes you smile.

I read a quote from someone that goes, "It is easy to get stuck when you lose your spark because then, you are stuck in the dark." So, I relate laughter to that spark, that strike of the match that ignites a flame that makes light. A good belly laugh ignites joy and smiling. Have you ever laughed so hard you cry, and then, after catching your breath, you say, Man, I needed that today! That is what we want to do today - remember something funny.

God Wink:

To say that my father-in-law was the best storyteller ever would not even come close to the detail and the movements and the facials that he would go through to explain a great story. He knew when to pause and how to get that belly laugh out of everyone listening. I'm going to tell you a story he told us. I know I won't be as good at telling it as he was, but it doubled me over laughing at his production of the car fire. Set the scene in your head: You're driving your Dodge Daytona over to a friend's house after picking up hoagies. It's a beautiful day, the sun is shining, the windows in the car are down. It's a great day...until you pull into the driveway, get out of your car, walk up to the door of the house, and as you glance back at your car, it is on fire. No warning, it just catches on fire. Thinking of grabbing a bucket and bailing water out of the hot tub seemed to be an idea, but the thought of the hot tub running out of water and burning the motor seemed a bad outcome. He runs up to the house, grabs the garden hose to extinguish the fire, and just like in the movies, as he is running back to the car with hose in hand with water coming out of the hose, he comes to an abrupt halt because the hose is too short. Trying to arc the water enough to reach the car, he is unsuccessful, while the car completely burns to a crisp. He runs to the neighbor next door to call the fire department, who did what they needed to do. (But my telling does not make for as funny a story as he told, so cut to the scene):

Friend comes home, and there is a car smoldering in his driveway. No one is around because Jerry left after this happened. He had called my mother-in-law to pick him up. Everything was a pile of ash. "I can't even find the keys," he tells us with his hands in the air, looking confused. My husband, Jerry's son, later asked if he retrieved anything from the car. Not missing a beat, he said, "I got my hoagie, but I never got to eat it." So as the story goes, a few days later Jerry is behind the flatbed which is there to pick up what was left of his car and take her to her ultimate resting place. With a glimmer in his eye, he says to us, "You know, as we were cresting a hill with the sky so blue, I'm looking at my car and thinking, How could this happen? A song comes on the radio. It's Elvis singing (and, of course, Jerry is singing) 'Mine eyes have seen the glory of the coming of the Lord...and we drive past a restaurant that she drove me to...He is trampling out the vintage where the grapes of wrath are stored...."And he continues on and on through the song barely able to sing the line about "I have seen Him in the watch-fires of a hundred circling camps"...and he continued in a soft voice "...and as we passed these places I knew that I would no longer be accompanied by my Dodge Daytona", he pauses, looks around, puts his hand on his heart and bellows, "Glory! Glory! Hallelujah His truth is marching on." And we all caught our breaths from this unbelievable, true performance. But throughout the evening, he would look around, laugh and sing again, "Glooooory, Glooooory Hallelujah...."

And that, my friends, was the award-winning performance played by none other than Jerry Niedentohl, who in my mind, was the greatest storyteller ever.

What is something funny you remember? Explain how it happened or where you were.

Mantra: *Today I will laugh and be joyful because you would want me to laugh.*

Windows

Windows, Windows to the past
Like Alice through the looking glass
you dance with the angels
As you have gotten your wings
My mind goes crazy
Just thinking these things...

My heart beats,
and yours no more
Each breath I breathe in
feels different from before

Each blink of my eyes
Yours forever closed
my hands move freely
while yours, forever posed.

The word legacy seems like a lot of responsibility when you think about yours. But when you think about all the lives your loved ones have touched, yours may seem small. Your person was just being who they were. They did the things that made them so special to you and to everyone that loved them.

God Wink:

This God Wink is about a young man I never had the pleasure to meet, but he is a true legacy in my eyes because of the words that he lived by: "Don't Waste Your Life." Bam... straight and to the point. Don't Waste Your Life...Now even though I never knew Brandon until after he passed, I truly feel as though I know him. Not in the human aspect but in the spiritual aspect. I can feel his energy and love every time he comes through in a reading. He was twenty when he suddenly lost his life in a car accident. I was contacted by his friends and family to do a group reading. He came through stronger than any spirit had ever come through. We laughed and cried. It was apparent to me that he made a difference in the world. The things he said to everyone who attended told me a lot about the man he was. His legacy lives on in The Brandon Tolson Foundation. A foundation created by those who loved him most. A foundation built in his memory to help families when they lose a child. Brandon's words, "Don't Waste Your Life", mean so much to me, and they touch my heart every time I think of him.

PAUSE...BREATHE...WRITE

What is the legacy you remember? What made them who they were? How did they touch the lives of those that surrounded them?

PAUSE...BREATHE...WRITE

Mantra: *Today I will continue your legacy. Don't waste your life.*

Please Always Remember
And Never Forget

Life's mystery is that I do not know when
My life on this earth will come to an end
Advice, I give, I hope to instill
guidance to help you climb life's crazy hills,

The many mistakes, that I know I have made
To help you feel safe, even when I was afraid
These thoughts I leave with you now
So, when I'm not with you, you'll hear me somehow

When the breeze blows the chimes
warmth on your face from the sunshine
Remember me dancing when the music played
And always remember, I'm not far away

As my spirit leaves this world in the flesh,
Having you in my life, I was so blessed
I'm sorry I must leave when you want me to stay
But God opened the gates of Heaven today

If before I pass, I'm in a strange mindset
Please always remember and never forget
I love you today, tomorrow and forever
And one day, my child, we will be together.

E veryone who walks in and out of your life is a gift. We learn new things from new people, and we teach those people as well. There is always a reason for meeting someone. . I do not believe in chance meetings. I believe in karmic meetings. The universe connects us with those we are to meet. Stop and think about the impact certain people have had in your life.

God Wink:

A close friend (brother) of my husband passed a few months ago. He was loud and funny. Hard-working, inventive, driven, and he loved God, his wife, family and friends. The man was ornery as all get out. He lived hard and fast in his younger years. Once he became sober, he would help others find sobriety, help them find a job or place to live. During his last days, he came to visit us at our shop in May. We sat outside for a bit. He shook his head and told me, "I don't think I'm going to be here for July 4th. I think cancer is going to win." I asked him if he was ready to go, and he said no, he needed to make sure his wife was going to be okay after he left. I smiled and said,"Then don't go anywhere till you are ready."He laughed in his goofy voice and went, "Okay, I won't."They had a second house that he wanted to sell before he passed to provide for his wife for a while. The second house had a contract for sale on it, and he passed just a few days before closing. He was determined that cancer would not kill him. And cancer did not. A blood clot in his knee took him quickly early one morning. Ty made such an impact on me that even after his death, he wanted to be sure his wife and daughter would be okay financially and asking several friends to check up on them after he passed. He took his vow of taking care of his family to the grave. Even in his death, he could still provide for them.

We all have stories like this. Think back to a story or a situation that impacted your life because of them. Today I will remember how you changed my life and how my life has changed now that you are no longer with me.

 Mantra: *Thank you, God, for providing for me.*

Everyone has a favorite item - something special to them for whatever reason. Things that our family and friends know to be special to us. Today I want you to think about something you know was special to them. What was their favorite thing?

God Wink:

As I pondered the favorite thing, there are so many, but one stood out. My mom had so many favorite things, her family and friends, her flowers, square dancing, antiquing, etc. But I'd like to think her favorite thing was something that I now treasure. My father gave her a silver dollar. I believe the story goes she was a waitress in a small soda shop on the square of our hometown. When they were teenagers, he asked her out on a date, and he gave her this silver dollar. I don't know if he left it as a tip but in my mind, I imagine him flicking it off of his thumb and index finger to her and Mom catching it smiling, knowing this was the beginning of a relationship that would last forever. She cherished that coin and carried it in her change purse until it transferred to my change purse. I remember every time she dug in there for change, she would move it to the side. I believe it always made her smile to see it there, as a constant reminder of the love they shared. Now over 60 years later, it is in my change purse to be carried until my last breath, and then one of my children can carry it and pass it down from generation to generation.

What was their favorite thing? What was your favorite thing about them? This could be a place, a color, a song, etc. Take a moment to write about why this stands out to you.

Mantra: *Today I am your favorite thing.*

The Hanky in the Top Drawer

The hanky in the top drawer
The one I held when you got your wings to soar
The one that wiped the tears from my face
It's your favorite; it's white with the purple lace.

Every tear it holds:
The hanky is filled with tears in the folds
For everyday you're not here.
I see it in the drawer, and suddenly you're near

Why is it so important, it seems so trivial?
This hanky in the drawer, a small white piece of material
But that hanky in the drawer
Has held me up those times I was about to fall to the floor

It was one you used to carry
The one that was in your hand when you got married
Given to you by your mother
But now that hanky in the drawer will be carried by no other.

Carefully folded in half then in half again
The four sides, like my love, it has no beginning and no end
How do I tell you how much you taught me, where do I begin?
It holds my tears and scent of your skin
That hanky in the drawer
The one I look at and it makes me miss you more.

Today, I remember watching you. You didn't know I was watching, but I saw you. Ever notice something that leaves a lasting impression on you? Today is about that lasting impression left with you. What is something you noticed that made a difference in how you felt about the person who is now in spirit?

God Wink:

 My grandmother didn't drive. My mom, sister, and I would go to her house to pick her up and take her for groceries and run errands. I was very young when my grandmother passed, but I remember vividly getting into the car; Grandma up front with Mom and Lori and me in the back seat. We wouldn't even be out of the driveway and she would put her arm up, resting it on the bench seat in the car. In her soft hand, there would be two handkerchiefs rolled up so that no one could see them. Knotted in the corners of the handkerchief, she would place 2 quarters. She would casually open her hand, releasing them for Lori and me to catch. I could see my mom's smile in the rear-view mirror. She saw what her mother was doing, but she never said a word.

PAUSE...BREATHE...WRITE

What is something you noticed when they thought you weren't watching?

PAUSE...BREATHE...WRITE

Mantra: *Today I will notice something special in someone and in myself.*

N o matter how much we love and respect a person, they have little things that drive us crazy. Admit it - none of us are without flaws. Today I want you to remember little things that drove you crazy. I know you would trade it all and would love to be driven crazy right now. Were they always late? Did they get stuck on something and talk about it over and over again? What was that one little thing?

God Wink:

Every year for Christmas, my father would buy my mom White Diamonds perfume. It was her favorite. It was not one of mine. Sometimes, the scent of it would give me an instant headache. She really knew how to wear the scent, if you know what I mean. It drove me crazy, it really did. I'd want to say to her, you have other perfume! Why not change it up a bit? But I know if I would have, she would have told me it is your father's favorite, and I'm wearing it. Then, she would have smiled and dismissed the conversation. Now that she is gone, when I smell White Diamonds perfume, it makes me smile, and needless to say, it is one of my favorite scents.

PAUSE...BREATHE...WRITE

Write about something that used to drive you crazy, but now it makes you smile:

PAUSE...BREATHE...WRITE

 Mantra: *Today I won't let the little things make me crazy. I will smile with gratitude.*

I n this memory I want you to talk about something they said that you remember. It doesn't have to be something that impacted your life, just something special to you.

God Wink:

 My forever friend, Jason, decided to leave this earth before his time. He was a rambunctious teenager stuck inside an adult body. Always full of life and quick with a joke. My husband, Jeff, knew him since they were kids. Jason was a few years younger than Jeff, but they played music together from time to time. When I met him, I was in my 30s. Jeff introduced me to Jason as Trixi, and from then on, that's how he addressed me. A long time ago, Jason bought a drum set from him. It was Jeff's first set of drums. When he was ready to sell it, he called me first. He thought it would be cool for Jeff to have them back. But money was tight, so I was unable to purchase it, but I felt blessed that he contacted me first. Jeff traveled with several rock and roll bands in the '90s and Jason thought that was cool as shit. (His words). He called Jeff "The Legend". I can still hear him laugh and say with a spark of orneriness in his eyes, "Hey Trixi, how's 'The Legend'?" or "Where's 'The Legend'?"

PAUSE...BREATHE...WRITE

What was something they said to you? Describe the body language they used, tone of their voice, etc.

PAUSE...BREATHE...WRITE

Mantra: *Today I will talk like you.*

ermanent imprints and thoughts they had and shared with us are stored in voicemails, text messages, letters and cards they sent us.

It's personal because these were thoughts they shared with no one else. They are ours. Our special quotes and advice.

God Wink:

I am a night owl. When I wasn't ready to go to bed or couldn't sleep, I'd always seem to get a message pop up from Debo. He was always a positive person. One of the last messages he sent me said, "shit when I'm dead I'm dead nothing I can do about it, but until then let's just have some fun in this shitty world we've become. I promised the good Lord to make people smile and laugh as long as he keeps me here and I'm having fun doing it."

Debo had been dealing with heart issues most of his life, but instead of worrying about it, his mission was to make people laugh and smile. And that he did.

"shit when I'm dead I'm dead nothing I can do about it, but until then lets just have some fun in this shitty world we've become."

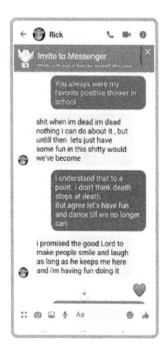

What was the message? Why is it so important? Today we are to remember these:

 Mantra: *Today I will send a note to someone in your honor.*

Come Walk into My Memory

Come, walk into my memory
I wish to speak with you
To hold your hand again
And hear you miss me too

Come laugh within my memories
So hard it makes me cry
transform these tears of sadness
To happy days gone by

Let's reflect the conversations
The advice you gave to me
I miss your voice, your smiling face,
You're who I need to see.

The things I took for granted
to touch your hand again
A simple nudge or sign from you
would help release this pain.

So come within my memories
I want to walk with you
and hold your hand and kiss your cheek
And say I miss you too.

There are times when we are doing something and we stop and smile because it reminds us of our loved one. This is a memory snapshot that I want you to transcend yourself to.

God Wink:

A high school friend that passed loved building trikes. Everyone always called him by his last name, Debo. His business name was Dingo Bikes. My husband and I set up every year for Bike Week in in Gettysburg. The year that he passed we were set up at Bike Week, I was walking over to the bathrooms, and I spied a cobalt blue trike like Debo's. I walked over to it and found a big duck feather on the seat. Debo collected feathers and built bikes. This was his way of telling me he was attending Bike Week with us. The following year at Bike Week, a man walked by in the crowd; glancing up, I noticed he had a tattoo on his arm that said "Debo." I left the booth, walked over to him just to make sure I wasn't seeing things and, yes, it said Debo. The day after we got home we lost our dog of fifteen years, Spike. A friend from out of the area just stopped by to see us after we returned home from the vet without Spike. While talking to us, he told us he had visited a friend and his dog, Dingo. Debo was letting me know Spike was with him. I smiled and cried.

What memory do you have that brings a smile to your face?

PAUSE...BREATHE...WRITE

Mantra: *Today I will smile.*

TODAY I RELEASE GUILT AND NEED YOUR FORGIVENESS

W ith death comes lost moments of saying and doing things. Reconciling moments that are no longer available to us. It sometimes leaves a void and a knot in our stomach to think we had plenty of time, only to find out this was not true. There are no answers to when or how we pass. When we do, those left behind try to find closure, which is sometimes difficult. What are you feeling guilty about? Death brings survivor's guilt. Guilt for not doing or saying something.

God Wink:

When my grandmother was in the hospital about to pass, I went to see her. I was about eighteen years old, and hospitals freaked me out. When I walked into her room, she was asleep, but she didn't look the same. I was afraid to wake her up, so I didn't. Saying and doing nothing, I just walked out. My regret is not waking her up to tell her goodbye. I realized that once she was in spirit, she knew I was there, and I also know she understands that at that age, I had a fear of death. My thought process was, if I didn't tell her goodbye, she couldn't leave me. She knows I was there and that I loved her. I now realize no goodbyes were necessary.

PAUSE...BREATHE...WRITE

Take a few minutes and write what you have regrets about. Is there something you feel you need to ask forgiveness for or is there something you need to tell them you forgive?

PAUSE...BREATHE...WRITE

Mantra: *Today I release guilt.*

Also with this chapter, I wanted to touch upon suicide and overdose deaths. This is a totally different type of emotion that we keep stored inside of us. I heard Sue Klebold (the mother of one of the Columbine shooters) say that she felt if love were enough, then suicide would never happen. So, love isn't enough. We cannot control what our loved ones think and feel. She added that addiction and suicidal thoughts from our loved ones are so well hidden from the outside world.

It is a "Stage 4" of mental health, and it is a tragedy. You wonder what is going on inside someone's head to honestly feel their loved ones are better off without them. What are their final thoughts before departure? How could we not see it? It breaks your heart, and you feel as if your own thoughts about this are fighting you. It's perpetual grief that goes through your head over and over again till you honestly feel your thoughts are trying to kill you. It is that circle of terror and fear that swallows you up. Then you shudder and think, are these similar thoughts they had at the point of their departure? You shake it off and cry, and the cycle starts over again. A lot of people felt the mother of the Columbine shooter didn't have the right to have these feelings because of what her son had done. She was challenged with understanding and compassion for her son and all the people his actions affected. But like I stated above, I was drawn by her quote of saying if love were enough then suicide would never happen. So, love isn't enough. We cannot control what our loved ones think and feel.

If you are the one left behind because your loved one decided to no longer be of this earth either by suicide or losing the battle of addiction, I'm sure you have had similar thoughts. I'd like you to take some time for self-healing, remembering if love were enough then suicide would never happen. So, love isn't enough. We cannot control what our loved ones think and feel.

PAUSE...BREATHE...WRITE

Take a moment to write about what has been reeling through your mind. Know that you may not receive all the answers but know that they loved you, and there was nothing you could have done to change the sequences of events that resulted in their departure.

Mantra: *If love were enough, then suicide would never happen. So, love isn't enough. We cannot control what our loved ones think and feel.*

The Reality of Life

I thank you for teaching me kindness and grace
when I dropped to my knees and fell on my face
I wake in the morning expecting you there
How do I go through all this despair

To know I won't see your face brings me sorrow
It boggles my mind how to face my tomorrows
The reality of life is someday it ends
so treasure each moment, events and true friends

People are placed in our lives for a reason. I truly believe that. There are no chance meetings. God gives us special people to help us learn or so that we can help them learn.

God Wink:

My forever friend, Deb, and I met in elementary school. I had just moved into a new school district in fourth grade. I knew no one. Most of the kids paid no attention to me when I was introduced to the class, but she was one of the first smiles I received when I entered the classroom. I will remember that smile forever.

PAUSE...BREATHE...WRITE

This is a special day to remember. This can be your first memory with a family member or remembering the very first time you met. Think about the time of year, where you were. Did someone introduce you? What makes that day special? How long ago was it? My first memory of you...

PAUSE...BREATHE...WRITE

Mantra: *I will start a journal.*

TODAY I REMEMBER SOMETHING YOU TOLD ME
THAT IMPACTED MY LIFE

Words leave strong impressions on us. They are lessons that last our entire life. Things we can pass down to our children and their children.

God Wink:

My Uncle Glenn would always hold my hand when he spoke to me. He'd look me square in the eyes and always say, "Oh honey, I love you. You are my very best friend." The impact this 99-year-old man had on me touches my heart every day. Tell people you love them as often as you can.

Take a moment and think of something they said or did that changed the way you think about things. Close your eyes: Imagine they are with you. Go back to this special moment. Do you remember where you were? What were you wearing? How the words and actions felt? Make a note about it. Give a detail of something they said or did that will forever be woven into your memory.

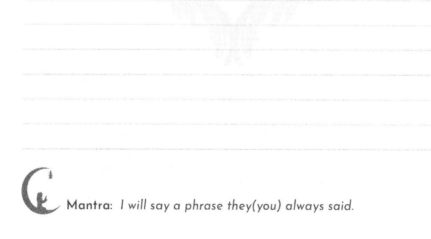

Mantra: *I will say a phrase they(you) always said.*

The car we drive says a lot about us. It is that trusted form of transportation that takes us to and from work, on vacation, to the doctor to run errands, etc. . In our lives, we can have many vehicles, but there is always one that stands out.

God Wink:

 Well, Mom had several cars. But the one I remember was a black 1961 Ford Fairlane she called the Tin Lizzy. I wasn't very old when we had it, but I remember the love/hate relationship she had with it. I remember how long the car was. I'm not sure why that sticks out in my mind, but it had the pointed fenders. I remember one time we were driving to the local pool for the day, and we ran out of gas. We were coming up on a stop sign where right across the road was a gas station. Mom told us to hold on because she was going to drift through the stop sign into the gas station. Luckily, no cars were coming. I just remember the smirk on her face when the car stopped in front of the gas pumps. Her famous saying for things to tell or not to tell our father was, "If he asks, tell him; if he doesn't ask, don't tell him."

Bonus God Wink:

 Another memory of this car that sticks in my head was when I was maybe in second grade, and we were driving home on a back-country road. Suddenly, in front of us was a hay wagon. Mom looked at me and said her father always told her not to follow too closely because the bale of hay could fall off. A few minutes later, off flies a bale of hay. I have remembered that for over 50 years, and anytime I am behind a hay wagon I think of this conversation. Who knew the impact that would have on me as a child?

What's a car memory you have?

PAUSE...BREATHE...WRITE

Mantra: *Today, I will take a long drive, play a song you loved and talk to you as I drive.*

- 124 -

 hotos are lasting impressions in each of our minds. They stop time so we can be transported back to that special moment.

God Wink:

 There is a photo of my grandmother sitting on her rocking chair in the trailer that sat on our land. She was holding our cat, Butterscotch. I remember the scent of her home. The way the rocker felt when I sat in it with the stool she made of High C cans in front of it. She made a lime green one and an orange one. Why I remember the colors is beyond me by in my head even with the photo, they are as real as the time I sat in her chair.

Place a
photo here.

PAUSE...BREATHE...WRITE

Things to do: Spend some time looking at photos. Go back in time to that memory. Where were you? What were you doing? Why is this photo so important to you?

PAUSE...BREATHE...WRITE

Mantra: *Today I will remember snapshots of you in my mind. You will forever be more than a snapshot in my mind.*

Time

Time ticks slowly without you here
How is it possible it's been six whole years
It was June, then July August September
these months are a blur, I can hardly remember

With each tick of the clock
My heart still in such shock
minutes to hours to days weeks then years
and all I can think of is wanting you here

As I'm lying here, alone in my bed
I hear the clock ticking, it is loud in my head
I want to wake up and cancel this dream
to have you beside me and see the unseen

To turn back the time
on the clock with the chimes
But the clock keeps on ticking
and ticking....
and ticking....

For this journal entry, I want you to remember a special time when your loved one had your back. They were there for you, maybe when no one else was there. They supported you and changed your relationship.

God Wink:

When my daughter, Megan was around two years old, she got very sick. I was a single mom with two children under the age of four. I had taken my son to his father's house so that I could take Megan to the doctor. I didn't realize how sick she was until the doctor told me to take her immediately to the ER for an x-ray of her lungs. He felt she had pneumonia. I called my mom on the way to the ER. I was scared and unsure of what was about to happen. Pneumonia still is very serious but back then was very dangerous. I arrived at the hospital, had her x-rays done, and when I came out to wait on the results, there was my mom sitting in the waiting room. You always knew it was serious when she would say that she left the house without making the bed. They confirmed what my doctor had suspected, gave me medicine and instructed me to wake her every two hours to see how she was breathing. My phone rang every two hours, and, yes, it was my mom checking to see if I was awake and okay and to see how Megan was doing. It was a very scary few days. Without the calm voice from my mother, I'm not sure how I would have made it through without crying the entire time.

PAUSE...BREATHE...WRITE

Now, I want you to recall a moment that stands out in your mind. What happened? What did they do that helped you? What advice did they give you?

PAUSE...BREATHE...WRITE

Mantra: *Today I will show love and grace to myself and to others.*

When you meet someone, there are things that stand out to you. The eyes and smile always tell a lot about the person, so I'm a smile and eyes person.

God Wink:

 When I think of those who have passed before me other things come to mind. With my one grandmother, it was how soft her cheeks were and the scent of Roses perfume. With my other grandmother, it is how soft and white her hair was, and it was always back in a bun. I remember, she would sing hymns like no other. Uncle Glenn's hands were wrinkled and soft but so strong at the same time. He always had a big ring on his finger that when he patted my hand sometimes hurt a bit. When I would tell him, he'd just laugh and pat my hand again and say they were love taps. My mom's smile lit up a room. Jerry's snicker and crooked smile appeared when he was telling a story. My forever friend, Deb's laughter was infectious. I recall Ty's loud booming voice but soft kind eyes. Debo's stance that could be somewhat intimidating, but he was a soft gentle giant. These are all things that come to my mind when I think about every detail of their faces.

I love these lyrics by James Taylor from his song, "Your Smiling Face". Every time I think of my mom, I think of these few lines:

Whenever I see your smiling face
I have to smile myself
Because I love you, yes, I do
Now I'm sure that I won't forget you
And I thank my lucky stars
That you are who you are

PAUSE...BREATHE...WRITE

When you remember your loved one, what do you see? Visualize them and describe every detail. What color were their eyes and hair? How did their hands feel? How did their skin feel and smell? Take a deep breath and imagine them in front of you.

 Mantra: *When I close my eyes, you are with me.*

Dreams

I dreamed you walked up to me
Something only in my dreams I could see
The things I always meant to say
You listened and talked with me today

The skies opened up with light
At the moment the world seems alright
The stars danced in delight
As I reached for your hand and held it tight

The flowers, so beautiful and bright
you smiled at such a wonderful sight
The birds were singing in the trees
your spirit was so warm and free

The pain you had once endured
Had vanished with waves on the shore
I watched as you walked out of sight
that day you gave up your fight

Each night when I close my eyes to sleep
I pray you are here and I weep
you feel so far away
till we meet in my dreams again one day.

Just a whisper away. That's right. Your loved ones are just a whisper away. They can hear you when you speak to them. Sometimes you may even hear their voice. You know those moments when you feel like you have a full conversation in your head with them? We often push it aside as our imagination. Thinking we just want to speak to them so badly that we make it up in our head. What if I told you that you weren't making it up? That they were putting their thoughts into the conversation? You are not crazy. They can have conversations with us. We just need to get out of our own head and allow the conversation to take place.

God Wink:

 I was speaking with a friend a few years ago when suddenly I heard my mom yell Stace. Out of habit, I put my hand up to my friend, looked behind me and yelled Yea? My friend laughed and asked me what I was doing. Apparently, she didn't hear what I heard. But as plain as day, I heard my mother's voice yell my name from behind me.

Today, I'd like you to speak with your loved one, either out loud or to yourself. Ask how they are. Tell them what you have been doing. Tell them how you feel. Remind them of your favorite thing about them. Whatever you want to talk about. Allow yourself to not overthink the conversation, just allow it to flow. Give yourself permission to listen to what your mind replies.

After you talk to them, take a moment to write a letter to them saying what you admire about them. Ask them to guide your hand to recall the details of the conversation. Whatever moved you in the moment. They are listening...they are only a whisper away.

Mantra: *I know you are with me.*

f you could hear anything from your loved one, what would it be? We always want validation that our loved ones are close by. We want to know if they have seen how our lives have changed. How we have changed. We do things in honor of them, but do they know? They see us and know what we are doing. Especially the things we do in remembrance of them.

God Wink:

I did a reading a while back and a father came through for his daughter. She was about to get married, and he validated he knew she would carry a picture of him with her as she walked down the aisle.

PAUSE...BREATHE...WRITE

Think to yourself, guide my hand and speak to me. You can start off by thinking: as I look upon you while in spirit, I see the tears you cry for me. I hear you call my name. I see you reach for the phone to call me. Now I am with you looking through old photos. I am here. I heard you whisper my name today. I was standing with you when the songs played, and you smiled and thought of me. It was me sending it to you. Although I'm in a different form...I love you, and I have not left you.

I'd like you to take a minute and ask them to write through you. I want you to write without thinking. What are they saying to you? Take a moment and write a letter to your loved one.

PAUSE...BREATHE...WRITE

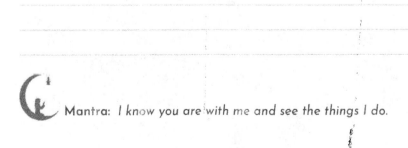

Mantra: *I know you are with me and see the things I do.*

Concrete Angel

A concrete angel in memory of you
When I need to talk that's who I speak to
Her face pointed up and the wing spread in flight
this concrete angel seems to make it alright

The concrete angel that sees all my tears
hears my stories and calms all my fears
She lets me know that you are here
This concrete angel seems to make all things clear

The concrete angel seems strong in stance
Takes my messages to you in a graceful dance
I imagine her telling you my thought and my dreams
this concrete angel isn't just a figurine

The concrete angel can never replace
missed moments with you in this time in space
I know you are with the angels above
But this concrete angel represents my love

olidays can bring a barrage of emotions and memories. We want to remember things that made these holidays special.

God Wink:

Holidays were always so important to my mom. When we were small, we would decorate the house with trees, place pine boughs everywhere. My grandma, and later my mom, always had a Santa's room. This was a room that the kids and grandkids could not go into, especially during the holidays. It was where Santa and the elves dropped off our presents. It held lots of gifts, wrapping paper, bows and bags. One thing for sure, Mamma Elf was an excellent present wrapper.

God Wink:

A memory that will always tickle me evolved around my Mom's Santa room. When my son was very small, he was upstairs and came running down the steps to tell Grandma he heard "footprints" in Santa's room. He is now over 30, and we still ask if he hears footprints. Now I have a Santa's room close to the holidays; probably not as organized as my mother's or grandmother's Santa's room. But the tradition lives on. Santa will always have a room in my family.

PAUSE...BREATHE...WRITE

Take a moment and write a special holiday memory:

PAUSE...BREATHE...WRITE

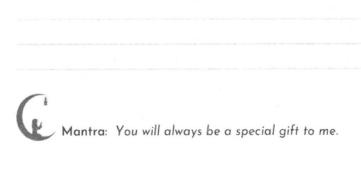

Mantra: *You will always be a special gift to me.*

We all have our own intimate relationships with the ones who have departed. We know things about them that we want to share so that future generations know them better. They may have guarded themselves in public, only letting people know certain things about them. This is your time to share a moment about something that others may now know. Your knowledge of something you'd like to share. It's not that it was a secret; it was just something you feel is important for others to know.

God Wink:

Uncle Heinz was the Chief Shipfitter on the USS Forrestal. At the time, the Forrestal was engaged in combat during the Vietnam War in the Gulf of Tonkin. This is a ship that in July of 1967 caught fire. This was something that he didn't speak of often. His words were, they don't want to know the complete truth. His wife, Aunt June, told me that she was on her way to the commissary when she received a phone call from her brother, John, to see if she had heard from Heinz. She was not aware of what was happening.

He had such a love of planes taking off and landing, Uncle Heinz was in the conning tower watching and saw what had happened. One chief grabbed a fire extinguisher to put out the fire, but a bomb detonated. Uncle Heinz, being in charge of the weld shop on the ship, had the idea to cut a hole in the flight deck to get air to the men below. The fire took 134 sailors and 161 were injured. The book Fire, Fire, Fire on the Flight Deck Aft; This is Not a Drill has several passages from my Uncle Heinz (Daniel Heinz Ringer) – a man that loved God, his country, family, the Navy and planes. I can't imagine the things he saw and heard that day. A true hero that never received a letter of commendation.

PAUSE...BREATHE...WRITE

What is something you'd like to share for future generations to know about your loved one? This is part of their story, their journey, their life that others may not know. Share their story here:

 Mantra: *Every path I take is important.*

The Legacy You Left Behind

When you departed,
it left me broken hearted
My house is not a home
I sit here all alone

The phone no longer rings
your voice no longer sings
My head is full of silence
I've lost my great alliance

I'm alone in my thoughts
to live, I know you fought
The things I remember
watching you dance at the community center

Your smile that lit up the room
and now you've gone too soon
As time goes by, my grief is resigned
I find strength in the legacy you left behind

THE
FIRSTS

THE FIRSTS

With loss comes new experiences. Every day is now different because they are no longer with us. It takes a while for the days to seem normal, even though they are never the same. As you walk through this, you'll have new firsts. Just like when a child is born: first words, first steps, first birthday. Your loved one is experiencing the same firsts as a new child. They are a new child in spirit. I want you to take the time on special days to reflect on memories and write how you are feeling. What you are doing. This is all part of self-care for you. Being able to express your feelings is an important step in healing. It's okay not to be okay. It is okay to be sad, angry, lonely. But it is also okay to be happy, joyful and at peace. I hope that putting your thoughts in this journal will help you move through grief and bring healing.

The first holidays and occasions without your loved one can be difficult, but let me tell you the seconds, thirds and fourths and so on can also be difficult. Let's remember how they made those occasions special. The person you are writing about took the time to make sure these holidays were important. Writing about it will help you remember the special moments. Not all of these holidays will be appropriate, and I may have missed some. There are blank pages for you to add anything that you'd like. These firsts are in no particular order because you may be in a different season when your loved one passes. Take your time. I've added a few extra pages as well if there are any firsts that you want to note.

Adding pictures of the occasion will add to your memories. Buy them a card and add it to your journal. The more you add, the more of a memoir you will have of them.

*T*oday is my birthday
I remember how you celebrated me by:

- My favorite gift you ever gave me was:
- We had a tradition of doing:
- My favorite memory of my birthday with you:
- Things you did that made it special:
- The silliest memory of my birthday:
- You made my birthday great because:
- Thoughts in my head right now:
- What I did today:
- If I could receive a card from you today, here is what I would want it to say:

PAUSE...BREATHE...WRITE

PAUSE...BREATHE...WRITE

PAUSE...BREATHE...WRITE

Mantra: *Today I celebrate my birthday knowing you are watching over me. Thank you for making a difference in my life and giving me a reason to celebrate today.*

*T*oday is your birthday in Heaven.

My first time celebrating without you. Something to do today: Say happy birthday to the stars.

I remember how I celebrated you by

- My favorite gift I ever gave you:
- My tradition for you was:
- The silliest memory I have of your birthday:
- I remember how much you loved:
- What I did today to celebrate you:
- Thoughts in my head right now:

PAUSE...BREATHE...WRITE

PAUSE...BREATHE...WRITE

 Mantra: *I will singe Happy heavenly birthday to you.*

THE FIRSTS

f I could send you a birthday card,
I would want it to say:

PAUSE...BREATHE...WRITE

PAUSE...BREATHE...WRITE

Mantra: *I celebrate your spirit. When I imagine the candles on the cake, you are now the ever-glowing space that lights them. I am blessed to have spent _ _ _ _ birthdays with you. You changed my life for the better, so today I will celebrate you.*

*T*oday is Valentine's Day.

- My favorite memory of you on Valentine's Day:
- We went out to dinner. You made this day special:
- Thoughts in my head right now:

PAUSE...BREATHE...WRITE

PAUSE...BREATHE...WRITE

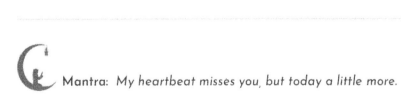

Mantra: *My heartbeat misses you, but today a little more.*

*T*oday is Easter.

- My favorite memory of you at Easter:
- Our family dinner:
- Where we always went:
- Thoughts in my head right now:

PAUSE...BREATHE...WRITE

PAUSE...BREATHE...WRITE

Mantra: *Just as the Easter Egg represents Jesus' emergence from the tomb, you have risen to a higher energy.*

THE FIRSTS

*T*oday is Mother's Day.

I celebrate you as my mother or I celebrate being your mother with:

- Things you taught me about being a mother:
- Thoughts in my head right now:

PAUSE...BREATHE...WRITE

PAUSE...BREATHE...WRITE

 Mantra: *I am flesh of your flesh. Bone of your bone. You are here with me, the best part of what made me who I am.*

*T*oday is Father's Day.

I celebrate you as my father or I celebrate being your father with:

- You celebrated me as your father:
- Things you taught me about being a father:
- Thoughts in my head right now:

PAUSE...BREATHE...WRITE

Mantra: *I am flesh of your flesh. Bone of your bone. You are here with me, the best part of what made me who I am.*

THE FIRSTS

*T*oday is Our Anniversary.

- Today we celebrate _____years together:
- Special memories of past anniversaries:
- Thoughts in my head right now:

PAUSE...BREATHE...WRITE

Mantra: *Our love is forever united never to be broken.*

THE FIRSTS

Today is the Anniversary of your Death.

- What I did today in memory of you:
- Things I want to say to you:
- Thoughts in my head:

PAUSE...BREATHE...WRITE

PAUSE...BREATHE...WRITE

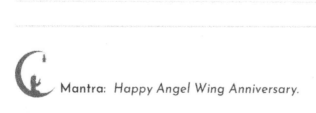

Mantra: *Happy Angel Wing Anniversary.*

*T*oday is Thanksgiving

- •• I am so thankful for you:
- • I remember where we went to celebrate Thanksgiving:
- • I remember what we always did:
- • Thoughts in my head right now:

PAUSE...BREATHE...WRITE

Mantra: *Today I am thankful you were a part of my life.*

*T*oday is Christmas Eve.

- • Memories that will forever be with me:
- • Places we went:
- • Things we always did:
- • People we shared the holiday with:
- • Thoughts in my head right now:

PAUSE...BREATHE...WRITE

PAUSE...BREATHE...WRITE

Mantra: *I will receive your presence.*

- 175 -

T oday is Christmas.

- . Favorite tradition:
- Favorite memory of you at Christmas:
- Ways we always decorated:
- Favorite gift I gave to you:
- Favorite gift I received from you:
- Thoughts in my head right now:

PAUSE...BREATHE...WRITE

Mantra: *You are the light in my heart.*

THE FIRSTS

Today is The New Year.

- I remember how we celebrated New Year's Eve:
- On New Year's Day we always:
- Thoughts in my head right now:

PAUSE...BREATHE...WRITE

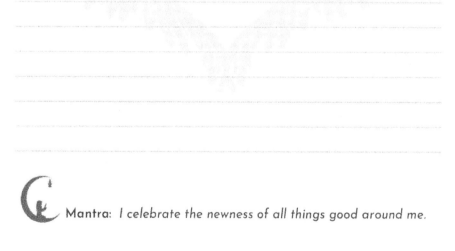

Mantra: *I celebrate the newness of all things good around me.*

THE FIRSTS

*T*oday is special, because:

- What I am thinking and doing:

PAUSE...BREATHE...WRITE

THE FIRSTS

Today is special, because:

- What I am thinking and doing:

PAUSE...BREATHE...WRITE

THE FIRSTS

*T*oday is special, because:

- What I am thinking and doing:

PAUSE...BREATHE...WRITE

THE FIRSTS

Today is special, because:

- What I am thinking and doing:

PAUSE...BREATHE...WRITE

THE FIRSTS

*T*oday is special, because:

- What I am thinking and doing:

PAUSE...BREATHE...WRITE

THE FIRSTS

*T*oday is special, because:

- What I am thinking and doing:

PAUSE...BREATHE...WRITE

*T*oday is special, because:

- What I am thinking and doing:

PAUSE...BREATHE...WRITE

TRANSFERENCE LETTER EXERCISE

Feeling the loss of someone can bring survivor's guilt to an ultimate high. Survivor's guilt is when we ask, "Why them, and not me?" but it is also the guilt we feel when we could not make amends or know the answers to why things happened the way they did. Whether you had a great relationship or a not-so-great one, guilt can be a never-ending tap on your shoulder.

For example: Let's say your last conversation didn't go the way you would have wanted the last words you said to them to be. This exercise can, if you are willing, help you face the situation and release it.

To do this exercise, find a quiet space where you will not be bothered. Turn off your phone and get ready to say goodbye to regret.

In dealing with anger, I want you to take a few minutes and go deep within the conversations you are having with yourself. Take yourself back in time to the moment of regret and remorse. I am preparing you to write a letter to the person and or situation. I want you to write without thinking. Don't worry about grammar or spelling. This exercise is to allow you to pour out all the emotions that come from your heart to your hand. Allow the words to flow through your pen.

Hint: you can start with I remember how I felt when....

State the emotions you felt. Why you said what you said. Or the emotions of how you felt when they said something. Recount the conversation in the letter. Tears, anger, sadness will come. Don't stop them. Don't push them down. It's you and your pen and paper. Get it all out. No one else is going to see the letter. It might be one page, it may be ten pages. Whatever it takes.

TRANSFERENCE LETTER EXERCISE

When you are finished, I want you to tear the letter out of this book. Take a breath and pray to release yourself from the tap on your shoulder that won't go away. Say to yourself or speak out loud (I prefer out loud), but it is your comfort level we are inviting. "I release you, and I forgive you. I release me, and I forgive me. You release me, and you forgive me."

Now take the letter, if you have a place to build a bonfire outside that is great. If not, a match and a fireproof bowl will work.

- Build a small fire if outside.
- Thank God, the universe and the person for the strength and wisdom you gained from the situation.
- Then light the letter on fire.

Remember, you are releasing them and forgiving them, as well as releasing and forgiving yourself. Watch till the letter is no more. This signifies that it no longer belongs to you.

If you keep the letter, it is still yours.

You are releasing it to God to take care of what needs to happen next. God is releasing you from these feelings of guilt, anger and remorse. He will take it from here. They no longer belong to you as you have invited forgiveness in.

If these emotions come back and tap on your shoulder, stop, breathe and say to yourself or speak out loud, These emotions no longer belong to me. They have released me. They are no longer mine to carry.

TRANSFERENCE LETTER EXERCISE

It may take practice as the mind can creep in at any time to remind you and try to pull you in. But if you are willing to work through this exercise, I promise you the knot in your stomach when these thoughts creep in will get smaller and smaller. And you, my friend, will get stronger and wiser each day. If new emotions come up, repeat the exercise.

I want you to know that your loved one, when they passed, had a life review. They have a better understanding of the situation, and they have worked through understanding why things happened the way they did. They feel no anger or regret, so why should you? They want you to live your life to the fullest, not with a speed bump that stops you in your tracks. Ready?

PAUSE...BREATHE...WRITE.

PAUSE...BREATHE...WRITE

PAUSE...BREATHE...WRITE

Mantra: *I release you, I forgive you. You release me, you forgive me. I release me, I forgive me.*

THE BRIDGE MEDITATION

Meditation to release guilt, anger and negative thoughts (you can do this meditation as often as you like). https://bit.ly/3osBHvx

I suggest recording yourself reading this or you can download it from YouTube at https://bit.ly/3osBHvx CLICK

Place a pen and this journal beside you for easy access after your meditation has ended. Grab a set of ear buds...

Relax - Find a comfortable position either lying down or sitting in a chair (not driving). You may want to place a blanket over you if you get chilled easily.

Take a few deep breaths just to relax. As you breathe in, visualize positive light coming in and as you exhale, release the thoughts of the day.

"Relax deeper and deeper with each breath. As you relax, calm your breathing down, slow inhales holding for a few seconds and totally release the air. Deep breath in again, hold and exhale. Connecting to your breath. Breathing in deeply, hold and release. All the thoughts of the day pass out of your mind with each exhale. Relax each part of your body from your head to your toes. Breathing in, holding and breathing out. Now, I want you to do a body scan. If there is tension in any part of your body, breath air through to the spot and release it. You may have a few, so continue to connect to your breath. Now envision a bright, white light above your head. Use your imagination if you can't see it. Imagine you feel the warmth from the light touching the top of your head as you breathe in and out. Touching your checks and forehead, breathing in and out. Your head and shoulders breathing in and out, arms and hands breathing in and out chest and back, hips and legs breathing in and out ankles feet down to the tips of your toes breathing in and out. Visualize that light going out through your toes down into the ground, forming strong roots to keep you grounded.

"Remember, you are safe and always in control. You may end this meditation at any time, But trust that you are safe to continue on. Breathing in and out slowly. In and out. Feeling your stomach rise and fall. Relaxing with each and every breath.

"I want you to visualize a white light going from the top of your head to the tips of your toes going down deep into the earth. Grounding you and supporting you. Do one more body scan breathing white light to any part of your body that is not relaxed and release any tension with a deep breath.

"Imagine the warmth of the sun on your face and a slight breeze in the air. The warmth on your arms. You can smell the sweet scent of freshly cut grass..

"Visualize your back yard. If you have a hard time visualizing, imagine your back yard. You know what it looks like. Breathing in and out. Look around, it is familiar and safe. Breathing in and out... deeper and deeper..... See the birds in the trees and hear their song. It is a warm summer day, but not too hot.

"As you walk around your yard, imagine yourself walking to the end of your yard. There is a beautiful meadow attached to your yard. You continue to walk, feeling safe and relaxed. The meadow is filled with beautiful flowers and butterflies, beautiful birds singing their songs. You feel the warm grass beneath your feet, and it is soft and warm as you continue to walk. The sun is warm on your face and arms, it is a beautiful day. The sky is blue, unlike any other sky you've seen.

"As you walk, you notice a small stream over on the left. It's not too far. You casually walk over to it. Maybe your shoes are in your hands as you walk over to the stream. The sound of it trickling down stream is so refreshing that you just have to roll up your jeans and sit on the bank to place your feet in the water. It is cool and refreshing, rolling over the small rocks and over your feet. A dragonfly or two buzzes by you, and you look at it closely and see all the brilliant colors of this tiny insect. It is a warm summer day, and you recognize how safe and protected you are. The sound of the water is comforting and refreshing. As the water rushes over your feet, you are going to imagine anything that no longer serves you washing down the stream. Just relax and breathe. Give yourself permission to release any negative thoughts you may have.

"Off, in the distance to the right you see a bridge. We are going to walk over to the bridge. Notice everything around you. The birds, flowers, sun, butterflies. The meadow is unbelievably beautiful. You can see and smell lilies, lilacs and honeysuckle. It is the perfect day. You are safe, and I am here with you.

As you approach the bridge there are three steps. Step up onto the first step and breathe. This step is for hope. Know that there is always hope. Take a deep breath and go to step two and pause. Step two is for love. You are so loved and have so much love to give. Take a deep breath and go to step three. Step three is strength. You are stronger than you think. I want you to trust in this amazing journey you are about to take. No fears, nothing stopping you. You are safe and relaxed. Start to walk across the bridge admiring the reflection of the trees in the water, the breeze on your skin... As you are walking, you notice a suitcase on the bridge. I want you to walk over to it. Breathing in and out ...in and out. I want you to kneel down and open the suitcase.

Click each lock and the suitcase gently opens. As you look inside, you notice that there is nothing in the suitcase. Right now, it is empty. I want you to give yourself permission to place any negative thoughts you have in the suitcase...take your time...breathe in and out. Anything ever said to you that made you feel disrespected, unaccepted, less than who you know you are.... place those words and thoughts in the suitcase. Continue to breathe in and out...in and out...Pull the emotions and thoughts from deep within you and release them into the suitcase. It's OK...you are safe. Go back in your memory of childhood negative feelings and emotions you have been carrying with you...place them into the suitcase. Breathing in and out...Think of elementary school, high school, college...release those events and emotions that have held you hostage for so long. Into your 20s breathing in and out. Release them, let them go. Into your 30s breathing in and out. They may no longer hold you captive. You have taken their control away by placing them in the suitcase. Continue through life events that have made you feel unworthy, unwanted, not good enough. These are the things we are releasing today. Always remember you are safe. You are only remembering these things, you are not reliving them. We are only remembering them to release them from your energy. Breathing in and out. There are events, people, and things that will come to your mind. I'm asking you to place them in the suitcase. Breathing in and out. Take your time. This is your journey. Now is the time to release anger...place it in the suitcase. Regret...put it in the suitcase...pain... put it in the suitcase. All the events that are quickly coming to your mind...you no longer need. You've been carrying them for too long. Allow yourself to place all these things that no longer serve you in the suitcase, things that have been holding you back...put them in the suitcase. If there is a certain person who hurt you and you need to place them in there along with the emotions behind the situation, place them in the suitcase. This suitcase can expand and hold whatever you need to release. You are doing great. Breathe...in...and out...in and out...slowly releasing all that no longer aids in your life.

Things that are stopping you from moving forward...place them in the suitcase. Take as long as you need. If you need to pause the recording for a few minutes, that is fine.

Now, we've placed all this stuff in the suitcase. You've transferred all your baggage into the suitcase. I want you to shut the suitcase. If you have to sit on it to get it to latch, then do so. Breathe in and out, in and out. You are doing great. Breathing in and out. I want you to stand up, grab the handle of the suitcase and throw it into the water... Let go of the handle. It is no longer your suitcase. Watch the suitcase float downstream. It is floating away further and further away from you. Watch it slowly sink into the water...breathe in and out, in and out. The suitcase is now at the bottom of the river, no longer to be seen again...no longer to be carried by you. Your slate is wiped clean. It's gone. Breathe...in and out...in and out.

We are now going to turn around, no longer attached to the suitcase, and walk towards those three steps. As you step down on the first step, that was for strength. What you just did took a lot of strength...you did great. Breathe and step down to the second step - it is for love. That is what remains. You placed everything else into the suitcase. What remains is love and joy. Down to the last step, the step for hope...there is always hope. God is in control of your destiny. You gave Him your baggage now allow Him to give you strength, love and hope. Begin walking back to the stream you had your feet in, and you notice your reflection. It seems lighter somehow. I want you to envision all the important things surrounding your life in the reflection as you smile and allow yourself to be proud of what you were just able to accomplish. Nothing can stop you from moving forward. You continue to walk through the meadow and the sun is warm, the air smells sweet. You have a skip in your step...a happy walk through the meadow with the warm soft grass below your feet as you slowly walk to the end of the meadow and into your backyard where you are safe and comfortable.

THE BRIDGE MEDITATION

You hear your favorite song on the radio, and you are listening to every note. Slowly start to come back and notice the chair that you are sitting on as you breathe in and out...start to hear the noises in the room and be aware of your surroundings. Be aware of your feet, your ankles and calves. Notice your hips and your back, your stomach and your arms, feel your wrists and your fingers your shoulder your neck and your head. Take a deep breath. Wiggle your fingers and toes and slowly stretch and when you are ready open your eyes.

Grab your pen and write about your experience.

PAUSE...BREATHE...WRITE

PAUSE...BREATHE...WRITE

PAUSE...BREATHE...WRITE

ABOUT SONGS

Songs can be powerful. They wake up memories, place snapshots in your mind, help you walk through grief, and they can be signs from your loved ones. Has there ever been a time you were thinking of them when you just wanted them close by and suddenly their favorite song comes on? That's a sign. They are letting you know they are with you. Spirit loves to come through in song. Spirit is a vibrational energy and music is a vibration. This is a fairly easy connection for them.

When we hear songs, they help us breathe, cry and laugh. I asked my clients what songs reminded them of their loved ones. What songs came through as signs? I've listened to each one of these songs. Some I had never heard before, but after listening to them, I understand why these songs were chosen.

I couldn't choose which ones not to list, so the list is rather long. They are all different genres and artists. Take a minute from time to time, look over the list and choose a song or two, find a quiet spot, close your eyes and allow your spirit, your energy, to encompass the music. Don't just listen to it, feel it. Allow the music to take you away from any chaos that may be going on in your life. Allow God and the angels to whisk you away, if only for a few minutes. Together, we can help each other through song and music. Your loved one is never far away....Just a song away.

ABOUT SONGS

- You are My Sunshine - *Jimmie Davis*
- Pocketful of Sunshine - *John Shanks*
- The Logical Song - *Supertramp*
- Amazing Grace - *John Newton*
- The Old Rugged Cross - *George Bennard*
- You and Me Against The World - *Kenny Ascher and Paul Williams*
- My Wish - *Rascal Flatts*
- Just as Though You Were Here - *Frank Sinatra and Tommy Dorsey*
- Don't Close your Eyes -*Kix*
- Make Me Feel My Love - *Adele*
- Goodbye is the Saddest Word - *Robert John Lange*
- See You on the Other Side - *Ozzy Ozbourne*
- Ave Maria - *Pavarotti*
- Grandpa Tell Me About the Good Ole Days - *The Judds*
- Feels Like Home - *Randy Newman*
- Homesick - *Mercy Me*
- I am Weary, Let Me Rest - *The Cox Family*
- Touch of Grey - *Jerry Garcia*
- Here Comes Suzy Snowflake - *Rosemary Clooney*
- It is Well with My Soul - *Philip Bliss*
- Go Rest High On That Mountain - *Vince Gill*
- I'll Fly Away - *Albert E. Brumley*
- Because You Love Me - *Celine Dion*
- Somewhere Over The Rainbow - *Harold Arlen*
- It's a Wonderful World - *Louis Armstrong*
- Wind Beneath My Wings - *Larry Henley and Jeff Silbar*

- Rise Up - *Andra Day*
- The Bones - *Karen Morris*
- To Where You Are - *Josh Groban*
- Blackbird - *The Beatles*
- 7 Spanish Angels - *Troy Seals*
- Greatest Love of All - *Whitney Houston*
- I Can Only Imagine - *Mercy Me*
- Remember When - *Alan Jackson*
- Three Little Birds - *Bob Marley*
- Have you Ever Seen The Sun - *Credence Clear water Revival*
- Tell Your Heart to Beat Again - *Danny Gokey*
- Jealous of The Angels - *Donna Taggart*
- In the Palm of Your Hand - *Alison Krauss*
- Tears In Heaven - *Eric Clapton*
- If I Ever Leave This World Alive - *The Flogging Molly*
- Beautiful Beautiful - *Francesca Battistelli*
- Heaven was Needing a Hero - *JoDee Messia*
- The Dance - *Garth Brooks*
- The Gift of Love - *Hal A. Hopson*
- You've Got a Friend - *James Taylor*
- Long Trip Alone - *Dierks Bentley*
- Jesus Take The Wheel - *Carrie Underwood*
- You'll Never Walk Alone - *Richard Rodgers*
- Where Rainbows Never Die - *The Steel Drivers*
- Rainbow Connection - *Paul Williams Kenneth Ascher*
- I Will See You Again - *Carrie Underwood*
- When I Get to Where I'm Going - *Brad Paisley*

- Knockin' on Heaven's Door - *Bob Dylan*
- I'll Be Home For Christmas - *Kim Gannon and Walter Kent*
- I Won't Let Go - *Rascal Flatts*
- If I Die Young - *The Band Perry*
- Ripple - *The Grateful Dead*
- Remember When - *Alan Jackson*
- Stop Draggin' My Heart Around - *Tom Petty and Stevie Nicks*
- Have I Told You Lately that I Love You - *Van Morrison*
- Angels Among Us - *Alabama*
- Who You'd Be Today - *Kenny Chesney*
- I Would Die for You - *Prince*
- Let Go - *Frou*
- Fear - *Blue October*
- Some Broken Hearts - *Don Williams*
- Help Me Make It Through the Night - *Kris Kristofferson*
- Daddy Can You See Me Now - *John Williams*
- Dream Tree - *Dave Matthews Band*
- Home - *Phillip Phillips*

MEDITATION TO CONNECT
WITH A LOVED ONE

(Do this meditation as often as you like)

I suggest recording yourself reading this, you can also go to
to https://bit.ly/3bSvwMn 【CLICK】

Place a pen and this journal beside you for easy access after your meditation has ended. Grab a set of ear buds...

Relax - Find a comfortable position either lying down or sitting in a chair (not driving). If you have something that belonged to your loved one, it may help if you hold it in your hand. I like to put my mom's slippers on and cover up with her blanket.

"As you relax, calm your breathing. Inhale slowly, holding for a few seconds and totally releasing the air. Deep breath in again, hold and exhale. Connect to your breath and breathe in deeply, hold and release. Let all thoughts of the day pass out of your mind with each exhale. Now, I want you to do a body scan. If you feel tension in any part of your body, breathe air through to the spot and release it. You may have a few, so continue to connect to your breath. Breathing in and out slowly...Now, envision a bright, white light above your head. Use your imagination if you can't see it. Imagine you feel the warmth from the light touching the top of your head as you breathe in and out, touching your checks and forehead, breathing in and out. Then your head and shoulders, breathing in and out, arms and hands breathing in and out, chest and back, hips and legs, breathing in and out, ankles and feet down to the tips of your toes, breathing in and out. The light seems to extend out of your fingers and toes into the universe.

"Next, I want you to invite your loved one to come into the light that is surrounding you. Imagine a figure in the distance walking toward you as you slowly breathe in and out. Notice your surroundings.

MEDITATION TO CONNECT
WITH A LOVED ONE

Maybe you are at the beach or your backyard or wherever you are comfortable. The figure is getting closer to you and they are surrounded in light and warmth. As they get closer, there is something familiar about the way they are coming toward you. You feel safe and loved. As they approach you, they reach out their hand and you willingly place your hand in their hand. You look into their eyes. Who is it? Pause for a minute as they come into focus. You may not completely see them, but you know their energy. They greet you, and they say something to you. What are they saying? Pause for a minute... Take time to listen and talk to them. Take as long as you need. Pause... They will back away when their time is up but know that right now you can visit with them and revisit again later. (I'll be quiet for a minute while you do this. You can also pause the audio if you need more time.)

When they start to back away, tell them something you've been wanting to say. Pause for a minute...(I'll be quiet for a minute while you do this. You can also pause the audio if you need more time.) Smile and hug them. Ask them to come back again. Watch until you can no longer see them.

Breathe in and out...start to become aware of your body, the room you are in, the chair you are seated in or what you are laying on. Start to feel your body. Become aware of your head and shoulders, arms, wrists and fingers. Move your fingers. Become aware of your back and your hips, legs and calves, ankle feet and toes, wiggling your and toes and ankles. Take a deep breath, and when you are ready, open your eyes.

Take a moment to write your experience. Do it now. Do not wait. Grab you journal and write down every detail for this visit. Write without thinking about grammar or spelling. Just write....

PAUSE...BREATHE...WRITE

PAUSE...BREATHE...WRITE

PAUSE...BREATHE...WRITE

WHAT DOES SELF-CARE LOOK LIKE?

Self-care is giving yourself permission to have compassion for yourself during your grieving process. Working through this book allows you to recall memories you shared that will be memorialized in this journal of remembrance. It is also to light that spark inside of you to help your heart understand what your head already knows.

We tend to rhetorically say I'm doing okay when someone asks. We actually want to say I'm lost, confused, alone, afraid, angry sad etc. But we put this wall up to protect our vulnerable side.

This is where self-care starts. It is okay with not being okay. Not feeling guilty when you have a good day. Somehow somewhere we were taught that when we lose someone, we need to wear black, carry the Kleenex and sunglasses as a security blanket. We were taught to hide from our emotions by doing busy work so as to not allow our emotions to surface. I mean, think about all the things you have to do when someone passes.

If they pass at home:

- Start with calling the doctor or nurse to verify them passing.
- Call the coroner and/or funeral home.
- Place phone calls to family and friends.

The very next day it's preparations for the funeral and your heart and mind are still in shock. Picking flowers and memorial cards, fielding calls, visitors stopping by the house when all you want to do is take a shower and crawl in bed with the covers over your head and cry. Your head is spinning, you want to be respectful to all involved, so maybe you don't eat right or sleep because there is no time to just sit and process what happened.

WHAT DOES SELF-CARE LOOK LIKE?

At this moment in time, it isn't about you - it is about them, which it should be, but if you don't do self-care the tidal wave of emotions will hit harder and harder.

Here is what I suggest before they pass:

- If given the opportunity to speak to your loved one about arrangements, do so. Record it if possible or write it down. Recording it, I believe, is a loving sentiment that you will have forever. Their voice stating their wishes.
- Ask them if there are any messages or things they want to say to those they didn't get to see.
- Take a picture of you holding their hand.
- Brush their hair or put lotion on their hands and spend some moments with them.
- Tell them things that stand out in your memory. Stories, songs, regrets...
- If there are things you didn't get to say, write them a letter telling them what needs to be said and have it placed with them.

Once the funeral home has arrived to pick them up, go take a shower or a hot bath. Just 15 - 20 minutes. This is your time to process what just happened.

Say a prayer and thank God for allowing them to share their life with you. And ask Him to give you strength for the days ahead.

Have a go-to friend. Call your go-to friend. It doesn't help if you don't call them and say I need you to help me. This is someone who can act as a "blocker" if you don't want to talk on the phone or see anyone. You're go-to person will hold you up when you can't stand. To help you make decisions if needed, (there are no right or wrong decisions at this time), tell you it's time to eat or take a shower but in the most loving way. My best friend and I made a pact that if something happens to one of our husbands, we will drop everything, go to their house, crawl in bed with them and spoon in bed for as long as the other one needs it. This is my go-to person. Just knowing she will drop everything and come spoon with me gives me comfort.

If you're not up to stripping the bed that they were in, it's okay. It can wait till the next day or the day after.

If you need alone time, take it. Turn off your phone and sit in silence. Do what you need to do for you. Eat right and try to rest. Play music and allow yourself to cry, don't hold it in. Self-care is for them as well. The way to survive death is through life. Slowing down and not making big decisions till a year after they pass. Getting rid of things too soon may cause you discomfort later. Ask family and friends to help even with the little things. Allow them to pick up groceries or clean for you. This is self-care for them too.

Talk about how you are feeling. Write about it in this journal or another. Go outside at least once a day and feel the sun on your face.

Try not to allow anyone to push you into something you are not ready for. Have your go-to person there to help.

Grief is not over after the funeral. Try to stay active but if you need a day in bed, take it. There are no rules, no handbook of what to do or not do. Just listen to your body, your heart, and listen lovingly.

WHAT DOES SELF-CARE LOOK LIKE?

To do:

- Have a go-to person
- Journal
- Warm Baths And Showers
- Play Music
- Go Outside
- Eat Right
- Sleep
- Time Alone
- Time With Friends
- Pray

If you still feel as though you have not walked through grief, these are things you can do at any time to help process what has been taken from you. But remember even though the body is no longer here, their spirit, their energy, their essence still lives within you. This is something no one can take from you.

Spending time in prayer and meditation will help give yourself grace for healing and time to process. Your world has just been turned upside down. It's not going to turn right side up in a week. Pamper yourself in self-love, time, understanding and grace. This will allow you to connect to your breath when you feel like you can't breathe. So, breathe, my friend, and be gentle on yourself.

Blessings to you for allowing yourself permission to grieve in your own time.

Each day of every month can bring new emotions. Here are some mantras and exercises you can do every day to help you walk through the inner journey of healing. Some days you may not want to do anything. Commit to reading just one line of these exercises every day. It will only take thirty seconds, and it can help you walk through your day little by little. Self-care is so important while grieving. If you don't take care of yourself, mind, body and spirit, this process will be more difficult.

Each month I have given you a theme. Every day of the week there is a mantra or something to do. Practicing these things will help you breathe every day. Repeat and think about these mantras throughout the day.

JANUARY
New Year, New Beginnings

Mondays: First day of the week.
Mantra: *Abundance is waiting for me.*

Tuesdays: Work on smiling.
Mantra: *I will think of things to smile about.*

Wednesdays: Self-love day.
Mantra: *I am who I am.*

Thursdays: Work on forgiveness.
Mantra: *I release and forgive you or myself.*

Fridays: Today, dream big.
Mantra: *Today I will dream boldly and dare to
 dream.*

Saturdays: Growth.
Mantra: *Today I will soar like a butterfly just out
of a chrysalis.*

Sundays: Day of rest. Meditation and self-care day.

FEBRUARY
Month of Love

Mondays: Love yourself.
Mantra: *I love who I am.*

Tuesdays: Love others.
To do: Today tell people you love them.

Wednesdays: To do: Random act of kindness day.

Thursdays: Prayer.
Mantra and to do: *Today I will pray for a friend.*

Fridays: Gratitude.
Mantra and to do: *Today I will tell someone thank you.*

Saturdays: Honor those who have passed.
To do: Do something in honor of your loved one.

Sundays: Day of rest. Meditation and self-care day.

MARCH
Month of Luck and Abundance

Mondays: Invite abundance.
Mantra: *I invite abundance into my life.*

Tuesdays: Give permission.
Mantra: *I do not need permission to be who I am.*

Wednesdays: Get moving.
To do: *Finish something you have started.*

Thursdays: Dreaming.
Mantra: *Today I will dream big.*

Fridays: Actions Plan.
To do: *Put an action behind the Thursday's dream.*

Saturdays: Help others.
To do: *Help someone with your time.*

Sundays: Day of rest. Meditation and self-care day.

APRIL
Spring

Mondays: Raise your vibration.
To do: *Dance before walking out the door.*

Tuesdays: Work on breathing.
To do: *Walk with a spring in your step.*

Wednesdays: See the beauty.
To do: Spend time with flowers. Either in your garden or buy yourself some flowers.

Thursdays: Thankfulness.
Today I am grateful for my accomplishments.

Fridays: Detox.
Mantra: *Today I will take a deep breath of fresh air.*

Saturdays: Patience.
Mantra: *Today I will be patient with myself.*

Sundays: Day of rest. Meditation and self-care day.

MAY
Honoring Being a Mother and Having a Mother/Grandmother

Mondays: To do: Today I will look at a picture of you and say thank you.

Tuesdays: To do: Today close your eyes, think of them and whisper I love you.

Wednesdays: To do: Write a memory on a sticky note. Place it where you will see it all day.

Thursdays: To do: Today text I love you to your child or someone that needs a mom figure.

Fridays: To do: Today text or call your mom or a mom figure to say I love you.

Saturdays: To do: Post a picture of you and your mom or you and your child or pet.

Sundays: Day of rest. Meditation and self-care day.

JUNE
Honoring Being a Father and Having a Father/Grandfather

Mondays: To do: Today I will look at a picture of you and say thank you.

Tuesdays: To do: Today close your eyes, think of them and whisper I love you.

Wednesdays: To do: Write a memory on a sticky note. Place it where you will see it all day.

Thursdays: To do: Today text I love you to your child or someone that needs a father figure.

Fridays: To do: Today text or call your father or a father figure and say I love you.

Saturdays: To do: Post a picture of you and your father or you and your child or pet.

Sundays: Day of rest. Meditation and self-care day.

JULY
Independence Month

Mondays: Anger.
Mantra: *I will release anger. It no longer serves me.*

Tuesdays: Guilt.
Mantra: *Today I will release guilt. It no longer serves me.*

Wednesdays: Forgiveness.
Mantra: *Today I will forgive myself and/or forgive someone.*

Thursdays: Hopelessness.
Mantra: *Today I will not give up on myself.*

Fridays: Kindness.
Mantra and To do: *Today I will kneel and speak eye-to-eye to a child/pet.*

Saturdays: Pride.
Mantra: *Today I am proud of my accomplishments.*

Sundays: Day of rest. Meditation and self-care day.

AUGUST
Chakra Month

Mondays: Root chakra. Red.
To do: *Focus on being grounded. Take your shoes off and stand in the grass.*

Tuesdays: Sacral chakra. Orange. Pleasure.
To do: *Focus on a relationship that brings you pleasure.*

Wednesdays: Solar Plexus. Yellow. Self Esteem.
Mantra: *I can do all things through Christ who strengthens me.*

Thursdays: Heart Chakra. Green. Love Compassion.
Mantra: *I love myself.*

Fridays: Throat Chakra. Blue. Communication.
To do: *I will speak in truth and love.*

Saturdays: Third Eye. Indigo. Intuition/Imagination.
To do: *I will be aware of my gut instincts.*

Sundays: Crown Chakra. Violet or White. Awareness.
To do: *I will seek clarity today.*

SEPTEMBER
Combination Month of Past Months

Mondays: Mantra: Today I will live one minute at a time.

Tuesdays: Mantra and to do: Today I will laugh out loud.

Wednesdays: Mantra and to do: Today I will find a peaceful spot to reflect.

Thursdays: Mantra and to do: Today, I will slow down and enjoy taking my time.

Fridays: Mantra and to do: Today I will tell someone I love them and give love to myself.

Saturdays: To do: Today, write a short note or text someone.

Sundays: Day of Rest, Meditation and self-care day.

OCTOBER
Fall, Regeneration

Mondays: Observation.
To do: Admire the colors of the leaves.

Tuesdays: Quietude.
To do: Take a moment to get quiet.

Wednesdays: Appreciate.
To do: Call a friend and let them know you appreciate them.

Thursdays: Complete.
To do: Finish a project you started.

Fridays: Mantra and to do: No worry for today.

Saturdays: Vibration.
To do: Today, play music and dance.

Sundays: Day of rest, meditation and self-care.

NOVEMBER
Month of Thankfulness

Mondays: Gratitude.
To do: Be thankful for today.

Tuesdays: Mantra: *I am thankful for my family.*

Wednesdays: Mantra: *I am thankful for my friends.*

Thursdays: Thankfulness.
To do: Take five minutes, write down ten things you are thankful for.

Fridays: Mantra: *I am thankful for the Sun.*

Saturdays: Mantra: *I am thankful for my memories of my loved ones.*

Sundays: Day of rest, meditation and self-care.

MONTHLY EXERCISES

DECEMBER
Celebration Month

Mondays: Mantra: *I celebrate and love who I am.*

Tuesdays: Mantra: *I celebrate and love those around me.*

Wednesdays: Mantra: *I celebrate and love those who have passed.*

Thursdays: Mantra: *I celebrate the guilt that I have released.*

Fridays: Mantra: *I celebrate the anger I have released.*

Saturdays: Mantra: *It's okay that I am sad you are no longer with me.*

Sundays: Day of rest, meditation and self-care day.

PAUSE...BREATHE...WRITE

PAUSE...BREATHE...WRITE

PAUSE...BREATHE...WRITE

PAUSE...BREATHE...WRITE

STACEY NIEDENTOHL

grew up in Greencastle, Pennsylvania. Since she was a child, she knew that one day she would write a book. Now, living in Chambersburg, PA with her husband of twenty-six years and her dog Roxy, she has been given the opportunity to write this book to help the reader heal.

She is a child of God, Spiritual Healer and a Psychic Medium. For over five years, Stacey has done thousands of private and group readings connecting clients with those that have passed from this earth. The readings offer a validation, closure and help toward healing spiritually and offer a reminder that our loved ones are still here with us. Through performing these sessions, one thing was clear: losing someone is different for everyone, but we all have a fear of forgetting. Nudged by her clients and directed by her guides, spirit and God, she created this book to help your heart understand what your head knows.

Stacey and her sister, Lori, are co-owners of a shop located in an old elementary school in Chambersburg, PA known as
The Hip Gypsy Emporium. Stop by!

Stacey is available for spiritual healings, readings, past-life regressions and mentoring. **Contact her** at

- ConnectingtoSpiritwithStacey.com
- ConnectingtoSpiritwithStacey@gmail.com or at
- 717-552-1840.
- http://Facebook.com/ConnectingtoSpiritwithStacey

CPSIA information can be obtained
at www.ICGtesting.com
Printed in the USA
BVHW040735130921
616627BV00033B/626

9 781087 908410